IMAGES
of America

ALONG ROUTE 1
MAINE, NEW HAMPSHIRE,
AND MASSACHUSETTS

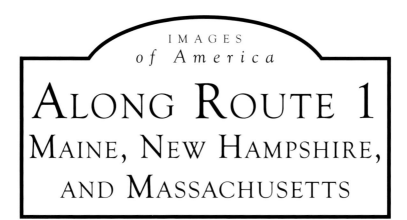

IMAGES
of America

ALONG ROUTE 1
MAINE, NEW HAMPSHIRE,
AND MASSACHUSETTS

Susan Mara Bregman

ARCADIA
PUBLISHING

Copyright © 2023 by Susan Mara Bregman
ISBN 978-1-4671-0995-6

Published by Arcadia Publishing
Charleston, South Carolina

Printed in the United States of America

Library of Congress Control Number: 2022950890

For all general information, please contact Arcadia Publishing:
Telephone 843-853-2070
Fax 843-853-0044
E-mail sales@arcadiapublishing.com
For customer service and orders:
Toll-Free 1-888-313-2665

Visit us on the Internet at www.arcadiapublishing.com

*For Berenice Abbott, Eleanor Roosevelt, and the other
intrepid travelers who explored Route 1 before me.*

CONTENTS

ACKNOWLEDGMENTS

Many people helped make this book a reality. Thank you to everyone who contributed a photograph, made an introduction, offered their expertise, or shared a memory. At the top of my list are the historical societies, libraries, museums, government offices, nonprofits, and universities that made photographs available for this project.

Special shoutout to Kevin Johnson, Chad Pelletier, Kimberly Smith, Al Churchill, Megan Pinette, Mary Peabody, Jerry Angier, Richmond Bates, Dave Gallogly, Karen Anderson Jones, and Madeline Soucie. Fellow authors and photographers generously shared images from their collections: Larry Cultrera, Mark Stein, Robert Cadloff, Andrew and Jenny Wood, Kristen Nyberg, Liz Budington, and Anthony Sammarco. Bob Cullen at the American Association of State Highway and Transportation Officials went the extra mile by contacting 15 departments of transportation to calculate the current mileage for US Route 1, state by state.

Thank you to my friends and family for hanging in there with me, especially David Dao, Richard Bregman, Fern Drillings, and Michael Bregman. Thank you to my dog for chewing up my first draft—you were right; it needed work. My editors at Arcadia, Caitrin Cunningham and Erin Vosgien, provided their usual expert guidance and support. Thank you for steering me in the right direction and trusting me to get there.

Thank you to my road trip buddies Liz Budington and Matt Denker, who willingly made crazy U-turns, parked in construction zones, sneaked into gated areas with me, and played endless games of Skee-Ball. I am grateful to Cindy Sragg, who looked after my dog while I was on the road.

This book drew images from many archives, including the following (shorthand designations in parentheses): Library of Congress, Prints and Photographs Division (LOC); Penobscot Marine Museum, Eastern Illustrating and Publishing Collection (PMM); Maine State Archives (MSA); Norman B. Leventhal Map and Education Center at the Boston Public Library (Leventhal/BPL); and Tichnor Brothers Postcard Collection at the Boston Public Library (Tichnor/BPL). Full credits for all other images are in the text.

INTRODUCTION

My earliest connection to Route 1 revolves around road trips between Boston and Maine when I was a graduate student. I have sweet memories of playing arcade games at Old Orchard Beach and then stopping for dinner at the Hilltop Steak House. For my road trip friend and me, the restaurant's attraction was not the food but the deliciously tacky ambiance and the knowledge that we were almost home.

But Route 1 is so much more than neon cacti and lobster pie. The highway blends historical gravity, Mid-century kitsch, and modern America without apology. US Route No. 1 was designated a federal highway in 1926 and today stretches from Fort Kent, Maine, to Key West, Florida. At almost 2,400 miles, it is the longest north-south road in the country. The road travels through 14 states on the east coast of the United States and the District of Columbia; this book focuses on the three northernmost. Together, Maine, New Hampshire, and Massachusetts account for a bit over 600 miles.

In 1927, the US Department of Agriculture (which was then in charge of the nation's roadways) described Route 1 as a "highway of history" and wrote, "The motorist traveling the road today is reminded frequently of the life and customs of the early days by the old inns which have survived the passage of time, and which now boast—in many cases with truth—of having sheltered the Father of his Country."

Photographer Berenice Abbott traveled the entire length of Route 1 in 1954. She took more than 2,400 photographs during the journey—about one per mile—and described her reasons for the trip in the prospectus that accompanied her prints. "We wanted to capture visually the character of a historic section of the United States, its beauties and incongruities and all," she wrote. "If visible evidences of the past survived, we wanted to photograph them before bulldozers and derricks moved in."

I traveled all of Route 1 in Maine, New Hampshire, and Massachusetts to document its sights and "incongruities," as Abbott would have it. I explored 19th-century fortifications and walked (very gingerly) across the Androscoggin River on a swinging pedestrian bridge. I climbed up slippery rocks to see what remained of an observatory that helped define longitudinal readings and found the marker for the 45th parallel of latitude.

I encountered a giant milk carton that marked an ice cream stand in Presque Isle, Maine, and a 40-foot-tall fisherman that once welcomed visitors to Vacationland. I played a few strings at candlepin bowling houses whenever I could; ditto for Skee-Ball. I ate a lobster roll in the easternmost town in the United States, dined at a tiki-themed restaurant, and sampled homemade pie.

I drove by neon signs in various states of repair. I saw the restored neon whale advertising Yoken's restaurant in Portsmouth, New Hampshire (minus Yoken's itself), the battered signs for the Red Fox Motel in Foxborough, Massachusetts, and the working sign atop Moody's Diner in Waldoboro, Maine, which is a replica of the original.

I encountered many casinos along Route 1, although most were not the gambling kind. At the turn of the 20th century, electric trolley operators built entertainment destinations at the end of the line to encourage weekend ridership. These trolley parks often had landscaped grounds for picnicking and casinos that housed dance halls, concerts, bowling alleys, movie theaters, and other diversions.

I heard from the daughter of the man who rescued Andre, the harbor seal turned celebrity. She talked about Andre with affection, the way one might describe a mischievous kid brother. The granddaughter of a motor court owner reminisced about playing shuffleboard with the older guests.

I watched the movie *Peyton Place*, which was filmed in Camden, Maine, and surrounding towns. Starring Lana Turner, the movie was based on a book so scandalous in its day that the Camden Public Library did not have a copy in its stacks. Speaking of scandals, remote Smuttynose Island was the scene of a notorious double murder in 1873 when an attempted robbery went terribly wrong.

It appears that George Washington did sleep here, and so did Eleanor Roosevelt. The first president is said to have spent the night at Lafayette House in Foxborough, or at least had a meal at the tavern. First Lady Eleanor Roosevelt patronized many businesses along Route 1 while driving to the family's summer retreat on Campobello Island, New Brunswick. She famously spent the night at the Royal River Cabins in Yarmouth, Maine, after the Eastland hotel in Portland asked her to kennel her dog.

But Berenice Abbott was right to be concerned. Route 1 is changing fast, and its quirky charm is diminishing. The motor courts and independent motels that provided affordable lodging for road-weary travelers are now mostly gone, and once-thriving restaurants have closed their doors. Sometimes, fires claimed a business; in other cases, proprietors sold their businesses. National chains are edging out family-run enterprises all along Route 1; I lost count of the big-box stores lining the highway.

Someone asked me how I would weave together the hodgepodge of sights along Route 1 into a cohesive narrative. But Route 1 is all about jarring juxtapositions, hidden gems, tenacious survivors, and tragic losses. And most of all, Route 1 is about change. That milk carton ice-cream stand in Presque Isle sits next to a chain motel. The Penobscot Narrows Bridge provides a starkly modern backdrop to historic Fort Knox. A colonial tavern in Portsmouth was home both to patriots plotting revolution and to slave auctions. Portland's historic Union Station was razed in 1961, and a preservation movement was born. Mom-and-pop business owners decide to retire after a lifetime of hard work, and suddenly a beloved local institution—maybe a drive-in theater or a bowling alley—is replaced with a car dealership. A lonely dinosaur overlooks the highway in Saugus, Massachusetts, the last remnant of a miniature golf course, while a giant cactus up the road is no longer attached to the restaurant it made famous.

The book follows Route 1 from north to south, and each chapter covers a geographic region. That said, this is not a guidebook, and the entries within each chapter are organized by theme and not geography. History does not always conform to geographic boundaries, and I occasionally used editorial discretion. I placed the Isles of Shoals in the New Hampshire chapter, for example, even though their history spans New Hampshire and Maine. Moreover, I sometimes put myself in the shoes of the traveler (who is not bound by arbitrary guidelines) and wrote about attractions a few miles off Route 1—including several seaside resorts—when they embodied the spirit of the highway.

This book includes a little of everything—from fortifications to racehorses—but it is not encyclopedic. Writing a book is a balancing act, and some roadside attractions did not make the cut. My goal was to be representative and not exhaustive. Still, I tried to capture the flavor of Route 1 in Maine, New Hampshire, and Massachusetts and hope that this book will inspire readers to visit and learn more about this highway of history before, as Berenice Abbot feared, the bulldozers and the derricks win.

One

A HIGHWAY OF HISTORY

US Route 1 (referred to as Route 1 and US-1 throughout this book) stretches from Fort Kent to Key West. The highway is almost 2,400 miles in length and is the longest north-south road in the United States. Today, Route 1 mostly runs parallel to Interstate 95 and passes through 14 states and the District of Columbia. (Photograph by the author.)

State Road
Calais Me

In the early years of automobile travel, highways were known by names, not numbers, and often referenced geographic features, presidents, and historical figures. In coastal New England, road names included Atlantic Highway, Lafayette Road, Newburyport Turnpike, Norfolk and Bristol Turnpike, and Boston-Providence Turnpike. By the mid-1920s, there were hundreds of named routes and trails across the country, and the result was a confusing mess. To help address the chaos, the six New England states approved a system in 1922 to assign numbers to roadways. The newly designated Route 1 followed the Atlantic Highway from Greenwich, Connecticut, to Calais, Maine. Route 24 continued from Calais to Madawaska. Route 15 connected Winooski, Vermont, with Houlton, Maine, via Bangor. Shown here is a segment of the roadway in Calais. (Courtesy of St. Croix Historical Society.)

A few years later, the US Bureau of Public Roads stepped in to create a consistent national system for numbering interstate highways. Working with state highway engineers, the bureau assigned numbers ending in one or five to north-south roads; east-west roads were assigned two-digit numbers ending in zero. The scheme became official on November 11, 1926, and US Route 1 was born. As originally designed, US-1 began in Fort Kent and followed former Route 24 to Houlton and Route 15 to Bangor. Then the road met the existing Route 1 on the coast and generally followed the Atlantic Highway to Miami, Florida. After the Overseas Highway was completed, US-1 was extended from Miami to Key West in 1939, and the road reached its full length of 2,446 miles. (Courtesy of University of Maine at Fort Kent.)

Baxter Boulevard (Route 1), Portland, Maine

Highways change over time, and state officials have extended, shortened, and otherwise altered Route 1 since 1926. Maine highway officials took Route 1 off busy city streets, including historic Baxter Boulevard (shown here), and merged the highway with Interstate 295 in Portland in 2007. Also in Maine, US Route 1 Business is a loop created in 1970 to serve downtown Damariscotta and Newcastle. (Courtesy of Tichnor/BPL.)

Route 1 still passes through Portsmouth, but state officials built a bypass to divert traffic from congested downtown streets. The 4.3-mile US Route 1 Bypass was a New Deal project and required a new bridge over the Piscataqua River between New Hampshire and Maine. The Sarah Mildred Long Bridge (shown here) opened in 1940 and has since been replaced. (Courtesy of Portsmouth Athenaeum.)

Today, Route 1 stays on the highway through Boston, Massachusetts. The road enters the city via the Tobin Bridge, follows Interstate 93 through the city, joins Interstate 95, and splits off south of Boston in Dedham. Early versions of Route 1 traveled on surface streets through Boston and were designated C1. The "C" stood for "City" and the term was apparently uniquely applied to Boston. Route C1 was rerouted to follow Storrow Drive and the Central Artery in the 1950s; the former is a parkway that runs parallel with the Charles River and the latter was an elevated highway through downtown Boston. After the C1 designation was removed in 1971, US Route 1 took over the segment south of the Charles River, while most of the segment north of the river became Massachusetts Route 1A. When Route 1 moved from Storrow Drive onto Interstate 93 in the 1980s, some of the roads south of the Charles reverted from numbered routes to their original names. (Author's collection.)

How long is Route 1? A 1927 estimate from the federal Bureau of Public Roads pegged the highway at 2,321 miles from Fort Kent to Miami. Some 363 miles were not yet paved, including 72 miles of earth road between the Canadian border and Ellsworth, Maine. The most recent official estimate came from the 1989 edition of *United States Numbered Highways*, issued by the American Association of State Highway and Transportation Officials (AASHTO), which logged US-1 at 2,593 miles long. To account for modifications to the route since the late 1980s, an updated (but unpublished) estimate from AASHTO now places the current length of Route 1 at just over 2,391 miles. Florida claims the most mileage (547.3), followed closely by Maine (526). Massachusetts has 86 miles and New Hampshire has 17. Taken together, Maine, New Hampshire, and Massachusetts account for 629 miles, or 26 percent of the highway's length. (Photograph by travelview–stock.adobe.com.)

Two

AROOSTOOK COUNTY

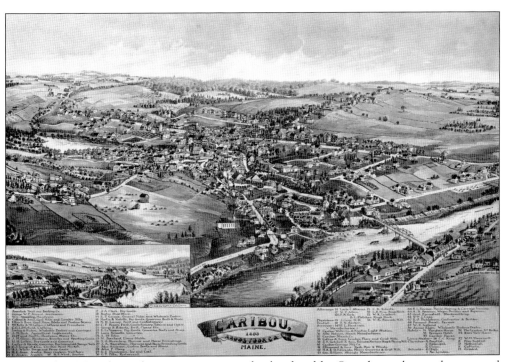

Aroostook is Maine's northernmost county and is bordered by Canada on the north, east, and west. At 6,828 square miles (including water), Aroostook County is the largest in Maine—about the size of Rhode Island and Connecticut combined—and is the largest county in the United States east of the Mississippi River. No wonder Mainers simply call it "the County." (Print by George E. Norris, courtesy of Leventhal/BPL.)

Fort Kent marks the northern terminus of Route 1. The official starting point (or ending point, depending on the visitor's perspective) is by the Clair–Fort Kent Bridge, which crosses the St. John River to link Maine with New Brunswick. Maine winters can be rough on painted wooden signs, and the Route 1 marker on the Edward Desjardins farm in Fort Kent was showing some wear

and tear. Here, a group of young women poses with the sign in this undated photograph before beginning to repair the marker, possibly as part of a project for the 4-H club. (Photograph by Velma T. Daigle, courtesy of Fort Kent Historical Society.)

In 1604, Pierre Dugua, Sieur de Mons, established the first French outpost in North America in what is now Downeast Maine on an island in Passamaquoddy Bay he called "Saint Croix." After a harsh winter when 35 men died of scurvy, Dugua moved the settlement to the more hospitable Port Royal in present-day Nova Scotia. French settlers continued to colonize the region, which they called Acadie, even as France and Great Britain fought over the territory. The British eventually prevailed and exiled thousands of Acadians between 1755 and 1763 in an event known as the Great Deportation. After the Treaty of Paris ended hostilities between England and France in 1763, many Acadians returned to their homeland, including the St. John River Valley in Aroostook County, where their influence can be seen to this day. (Photograph by George French, courtesy of MSA.)

"This is the forest primeval." So begins *Evangeline, A Tale of Acadie*, the 1847 epic poem by Henry Wadsworth Longfellow. The poem follows fictional Acadian lovers Evangeline and Gabriel who were separated during the deportation. Evangeline spends the rest of her life searching for her lost love. Finally, as an old woman in Philadelphia tending the sick, she finds Gabriel on his deathbed. They connect for a moment, and he dies in her arms. (Courtesy of LOC.)

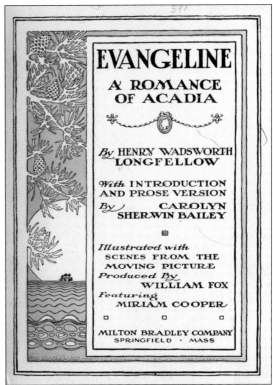

Acadian Village opened in Van Buren on July 1, 1976, just in time to be named Maine's best bicentennial project. The village honors Acadian culture with a collection of 17 historic buildings, some relocated and some recreated on-site, including a chapel, schoolhouse, blacksmith shop, barn, and several residences. This statue pays homage to Evangeline. (Courtesy of National Park Service.)

The border between Maine and New Brunswick was still disputed in the 1830s, and tensions between the American and British governments were high. Fort Kent was built in 1838 to shore up Maine's northern defenses for what became known as the Aroostook War. The war began as a skirmish between armed lumberjacks in Caribou and had no casualties except for an ill-fated bear. The war ended when the Webster-Ashburton Treaty defined the United States–Canada border in 1842. Fort Kent was abandoned a year later. The blockhouse, which was the only structure to survive, became a private residence in 1857 when Mary Page purchased it from the State of Maine for $250 and called it home for 33 years. Fort Kent was returned to the state in 1891 and designated a national historic landmark in 1973. Today, local Eagle Scouts manage the site in cooperation with the state. (Photograph by George French, courtesy of MSA.)

Spanning nearly 100 miles along Route 1 from Presque Isle to Topsfield, the Maine Solar System Model was the brainchild of Kevin McCartney, a professor at the University of Maine at Presque Isle. About 700 volunteers built the steel and fiberglass planets between 1999 and 2003; they are mounted on poles along the road. The scale model uses one mile to represent an astronomical unit (93 million miles). (Courtesy of University of Maine at Presque Isle.)

On August 11, 1978, Ben Abruzzo, Maxie Anderson, and Larry Newman took off from Presque Isle in a helium-filled balloon. On August 17, the *Double Eagle II* landed in a wheat field in France, marking the first successful transatlantic crossing by a crewed balloon. A park in Presque Isle commemorates the event with a replica of the balloon. (Courtesy of Smithsonian National Air and Space Museum, NASM 7A43915.)

Aroostook County farmers began growing potatoes in the early 1800s, but the arrival of the Bangor and Aroostook Railroad at the end of the 19th century brought Maine potatoes to the world. By the 1940s, Maine led the United States in potato production, and the red, white, and blue freight cars were a familiar sight. (Courtesy of Bangor Public Library.)

But the Bangor and Aroostook did more than move potatoes. The railroad carried passengers—and sometimes a little more. Train No. 22, which originated near the Canadian border in Fort Kent, was an easy way to sneak booze into the country. To avoid detection during Customs inspections, passengers on the so-called "gin train" would hang the contraband bottles out the window. (Photograph by Howard Moulton, courtesy of University of Maine at Fort Kent.)

About 3,500 German prisoners of war were housed at Camp Houlton between July 1944 and May 1946. Many POWs worked at local farms where they planted and picked potatoes, beans, peas, and corn for a dollar a day. They also took advantage of the camp's art program, and some of their paintings are on display in Houlton today. (Courtesy of the Aroostook County Historical and Art Museum.)

The Office of Civil and Defense Mobilization was a short-lived federal program initiated in 1958 to organize and support the nation's nonmilitary defense activities. Here, civil defense volunteers in Presque Isle rescue a "lost" hunter during a test conducted for Maine and New Brunswick officials. The program disbanded in 1973. (Courtesy of National Archives, 7385138.)

The Potato Blossom Festival was first held in the 1930s in Aroostook County and settled into its permanent home in Fort Fairfield in 1947. Valeska Ward Lombard was crowned the first Miss Potato Blossom in 1936, an honor she never took seriously, according to published reports. The 2022 festival marked 75 years of celebrating Maine's favorite crop in Fort Fairfield. (Photograph by George French, courtesy of MSA.)

In 1959, the national Christmas tree came from Presque Isle. The 70-foot tall white spruce was shipped to Washington, DC, on two Bangor and Aroostook Railroad flatcars. After arriving in the capital, the tree was decorated with 3,800 lights. The event marked the Maine city's centennial. (Courtesy of Presque Isle Historical Society.)

The entire population of Presque Isle seemed to turn out for the October 1940 potato barrel rolling contest. According to an advertising flyer, newsreel photographers from Paramount and Fox were on hand to record the event. Here, schoolgirls brandish potatoes as part of the day's festivities. (Photograph by Jack Delano, courtesy of LOC, FSA/OWI Collection, LC-USF34-041763-D.)

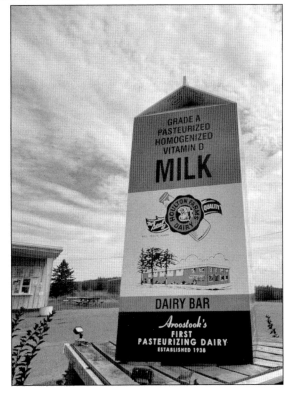

Mike Clark started Houlton Farms Dairy in 1938; it was the first dairy in Aroostook County to pasteurize its milk, and milkmen delivered the company's products to local households until 1974. The Lincoln family bought the dairy in 1982 and still owns it. Shown here is the Houlton Farms Dairy Bar in Presque Isle with its eye-catching milk carton, one of three ice-cream stands opened in the early 1980s. (Photograph by the author.)

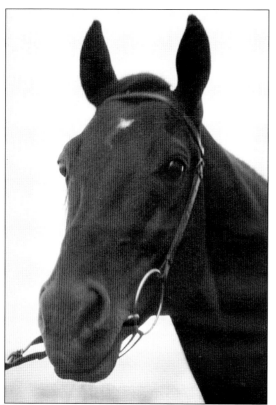

John R. Braden was a racehorse with his own bank account. The Mooseleuk Club of Presque Isle purchased the standardbred for about $4,000 in 1921. The trotter competed in Maine and the Canadian Maritimes and was almost impossible to beat. Nicknamed "the Little Iron Horse" and "Cock of the North," John R. Braden earned about $48,000 during his career, and the city set up a bank account in his name to deposit the purses. The Northeastland Hotel in Presque Isle (shown here) was the scene of one of John R. Braden's most famous off-track exploits. On October 14, 1921, guests gathered at the hotel to celebrate Braden's success. They led the horse inside and served him oats in a silver bowl. John R. Braden made his last appearance in 1927 and was able to retire in style, thanks to the banked winnings. The Little Iron Horse died in 1929 at the age of 17. In 1950, the Braden Theater opened, named in honor of Presque Isle's favorite equine. (Left, courtesy of Presque Isle Historical Society; below, courtesy of PMM, LB2010.9.120783.)

Three

DOWNEAST

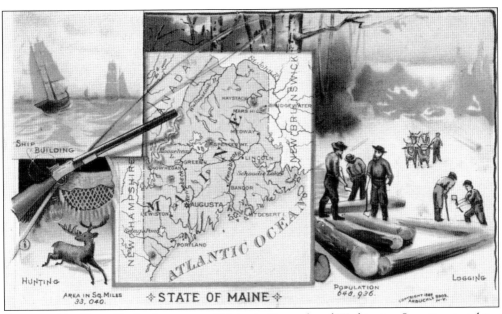

Downeast (also Down East) refers to coastal Maine in Hancock and Washington Counties, stretching from Penobscot Bay to the Canadian border. The term is a nautical reference; ships sailing from Boston were said to travel downwind in a northeasterly direction. The region is known for its rocky coastline and wild blueberry harvests. The first naval battle in the Revolutionary War took place in Machias, and Maine's sardine industry was once centered in Eastport and Lubec. (Courtesy of Leventhal/BPL.)

MARKER ON U. S. 1 in WASHINGTON COUNTY, MAINE

The 45th parallel is a line of latitude that marks the distance halfway between the Equator and the North Pole. In 1888, two surveyors identified the location in Perry where the latitude line passed through a house; they used a brass pin to mark the spot. The Perry townspeople commissioned a granite monument in 1896 which, upon its dedication on July 4, 1899, became the first 45th parallel marker in the United States. (Courtesy of St. Croix Historical Society.)

In 1857, the US Coast and Geodetic Survey, a predecessor to the National Oceanic and Atmospheric Administration (NOAA), established the Calais Observatory to conduct astronomical observations. The work of the observatory led to the precise determination of longitude in Cambridge, Massachusetts, in relation to Greenwich, England. Today, two granite stones that once held scientific instruments remain on the site, which became the first location on the NOAA Heritage Trail in 2005. (Photograph by the author.)

HANCOCK-SULLIVAN, ME. BRIDGE. 2.

The Hancock-Sullivan Bridge opened in 1926, replacing the Waukeag ferry that connected the towns. The span was known as the "Singing Bridge" because of the noise it made when cars drove over its steel mesh roadway. The bridge was replaced in 1999 with a concrete structure that no longer sang. (Courtesy of PMM, LB2008.19.116231.)

James Shepherd Pike was a businessman and journalist born in Calais in 1811. Sometime around 1870, he erected 12 granite markers at one-mile intervals along what is now Route 1 between his home in Robbinston and his business interests in Calais. According to local lore, Pike used the markers to time the performance of his horses. (Photograph by the author.)

Many associate Maine with lobsters, but sardine canneries were a mainstay of the Downeast economy for over 100 years. The first cannery opened in Eastport in the 1870s, and the last one closed in Prospect Harbor in 2010. The industry was centered in Eastport and Lubec and stretched along Maine's Atlantic coast. In the early 1900s, more than 8,000 people worked at 89 canneries. Investigative photographer Lewis Hine documented child labor practices at the start of the 20th century. His influential photographs showed children working in factories, farms, canneries, and sweatshops. Shown here are young "cartoners" at a cannery in Eastport in 1911; they were responsible for putting cans of sardines into paper cartons. Most were under 12 years old. (Photograph by Lewis Wickes Hine, courtesy of the National Child Labor Committee collection, LOC.)

A 40-foot tall sign known as "Sardine Man" or "Big Jim" once stood in Kittery. The giant fisherman carried a sardine can that read "Maine Sardines Welcome You to Vacationland & Sardineland." When the Maine Sardine Council took down the sign in the 1980s, Stinson Seafoods repurposed Big Jim to promote its cannery in Prospect Harbor. Big Jim stuck around when a lobster processor took over the plant in 2010, but he swapped the sardine can for a lobster trap. (Photograph by the author.)

About 10 miles off Route 1 in Jonesport, the Maine Coast Sardine History Museum documents the state's sardine industry. The museum reflects the vision of Ronnie and Mary Peabody, who collected sardine memorabilia for years; they built the museum next to their home in 2005. The collection includes artifacts from the once-thriving industry, including a display of scissors, each one tagged with the name of the woman who used it when processing sardines. (Courtesy of Tides Institute and Museum of Art.)

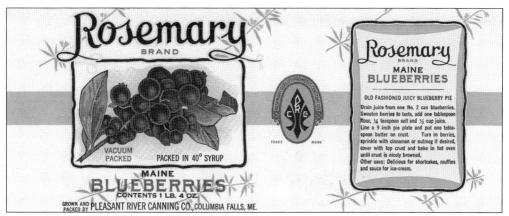

Native to North America, the wild blueberry has thrived in the harsh climate and rocky terrain of Maine and eastern Canada for millennia. Maine's Native Americans relied on the berries for food and medicine, and many believed the fruit had magical powers. Wild blueberries were first harvested commercially in Maine during the Civil War, when the canned berries fed Union soldiers. (Courtesy of Tides Institute and Museum of Art.)

In 1946, the University of Maine purchased 30 acres in Jonesboro for a research facility named Blueberry Hill Farm. Research at the farm and on campus has supported the growth of Maine's wild blueberry industry. Shown here is a demonstration of equipment for burning wild blueberry fields, which was the traditional technique for pruning. (Courtesy of Special Collections, Raymond H. Fogler Library, University of Maine.)

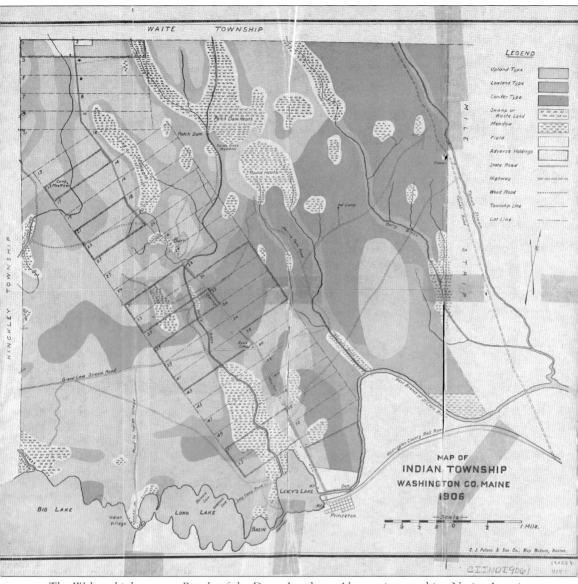

The Wabanaki, known as People of the Dawn Land, are Algonquian-speaking Native Americans with traditional homelands in northern New England and maritime Canada. Maine is home to five federally recognized Wabanaki tribes; most have tribal villages near Route 1. The Aroostook Band of Micmac (also Mi'kmaq) is centered around Presque Isle in Aroostook County. The Houlton Band of Maliseet Indians calls the Meduxnekeag River home and has tribal offices in Littleton in Aroostook County. Passamaquoddy Bay was the ancestral homeland of the Passamaquoddy Tribe. The tribe has two distinct self-governing communities in Maine at Sipayik (Pleasant Point) and Indian Township; both are in Washington County. Finally, the people of the Penobscot Nation have traditionally inhabited the land along the Penobscot River and its tributaries. Their primary village is in Penobscot County on Indian Island near Old Town. This map shows Indian Township in 1906. (Map by C.J. Peters, courtesy of Maine State Library.)

Burnham Tavern is a historic building in Machias known for its connection with the Battle of Machias, the first naval engagement in the Revolutionary War. In June 1775, the settlers in Machias were faced with an impossible choice. The British armed sloop HMS *Margaretta* threatened to cut off food supplies unless the townspeople supplied lumber to build barracks for British troops in Boston. Meeting at Burnham Tavern, the locals debated their options and chose to fight back. On June 12 (just days before the Battle of Bunker Hill), the colonists captured the *Margaretta*. When the fighting stopped, the tavern was used as a hospital to treat the wounded on both sides. Today, the Daughters of the American Revolution manage the Burnham Tavern Museum. (Photograph by Josiah T. Tubby, courtesy of LOC, HABS ME, 15-MACH,1-.)

The Pope Memorial Bridge crossed the East Machias River and was the first reinforced concrete arch bridge constructed in Maine. Civil engineer Leonard Metcalf designed the three-arch structure, which replaced an earlier wooden bridge in 1902 (although the dedication plaque claims 1909). The bridge was financed by descendants of William Pope, a prominent resident of East Machias in the 1800s. (Photograph by Brian Vanden Brink, courtesy of LOC, HAER MA, 15-MACHE,1-.)

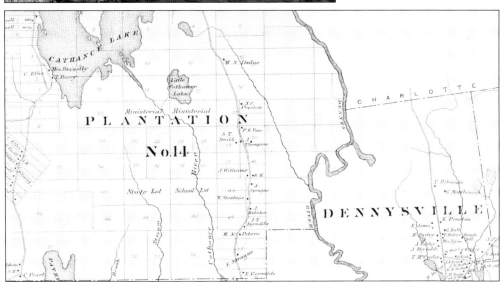

Maine has plantations, but they have nothing in common with those in the American South. In Maine, a plantation is a form of local government similar to a town and is usually seen in rural areas. This detail from an 1881 map shows Plantation 14, near Dennysville; today, the state has about 30 plantations. (Courtesy of MSA.)

Jennie and Smitty Thomas opened the International Motel in Calais in 1955. The name is apt; the accommodations are less than a mile from the United States–Canada border crossing. The neon arrow is now gone, but the motel is still in the family. (Courtesy of St. Croix Historical Society.)

Residents on both sides of the St. Croix River cheered when the Ferry Point "steel bridge" linked Calais with St. Stephen, New Brunswick, in 1895. Previous spans had charged a toll for crossing between the United States and Canada. But the new bridge was designed to carry streetcars, and it was no longer feasible to collect tolls. Finally, residents could cross the bridge for free. (Courtesy of PMM, LB2007.1.114244.)

Pierre Dugua's 1604 settlement on Saint Croix Island marked the beginning of a French presence in North America. Although the settlement failed, the island was designated as the Saint Croix Island International Historic Site in 1984. Public access to the island is restricted, but the National Park Service and Parks Canada maintain interpretive sites in Calais and Bayside, New Brunswick, respectively. (Photograph by the author.)

The Schoodic National Scenic Byway encourages motorists to experience the sights and culture in this part of Downeast Maine. The 29-mile roadway travels along Route 1 in Hancock and Sullivan and leaves the highway to take visitors into Winter Harbor and Acadia National Park. (Photograph by the author.)

A detour from Route 1, Acadia National Park comprises about 49,000 acres on Mount Desert Island, part of the Schoodic Peninsula, and several other islands. The park was first known as Sieur de Monts National Monument in 1916 (after Pierre Dugua, who led the first European settlement in North America) and then designated Lafayette National Park in 1919. The park received its current name in 1929 in honor of the former French colony of Acadie. Acadia was the first national park to be established east of the Mississippi River and the first to be created from private land gifted to the public. The visionaries who helped build Acadia included Charles W. Eliot, George B. Dorr, and John D. Rockefeller. Dorr is shown here in the park on snowshoes. (Courtesy of National Park Service/Acadia National Park.)

Construction began on Fort Knox in 1844 and continued until Congress stopped funding the not-quite-complete fortification in 1869. Located in Prospect, Fort Knox was intended to protect the Penobscot River valley against potential invasions by sea, but never saw combat. The federal government decommissioned the fort in 1923, and the State of Maine purchased the site. The granite fort is considered one of the best-preserved military fortifications on the New England coast and was named a national historic landmark in 1970. (Courtesy of PMM, LB2007.1.72020.)

A blue geodesic dome welcomes visitors to Wild Blueberry Land in Columbia Falls. The blueberry-themed park celebrates Maine's official fruit and educates visitors about the benefits of small family farms. Dell and Marie Emerson opened the exhibit in 2001. Dell was a researcher at Blueberry Hill Farm, and Marie is a baker and educator. Together, they tend their 220-acre Wild Wescogus Berries farm and create and sell blueberry treats. (Photograph by the author.)

Route 1 no longer passes through Bangor, but a monument to the city's favorite son would fit right in with the highway's over-the-top attractions. Bangor claims to be the birthplace of Paul Bunyan (as does Minnesota), and a 31-foot statue of the lumberjack overlooks Main Street. The fiberglass likeness was created by Maine artist Normand Martin and unveiled in 1959 on Bunyan's 125th birthday (according to the birth certificate displayed in city hall). (Photograph by the author.)

Ray Murphy made his first piece of chainsaw art in 1952 when he was 10 years old. He brought his sawyer skills to Maine in 1989 and began offering "chainsaw sawyer artist live shows" in Hancock in 2006. Murphy retired from the shows in 2019 but is still creating chainsaw art. (Photograph by the author.)

In the 1920s, motorists driving along the Maine seacoast had to cross the Penobscot River by ferry or take an inland detour through Bangor. When the ferry could no longer keep up with traffic growth, the state built a new bridge between Prospect and Verona Island. The Waldo-Hancock Bridge (shown here) opened on November 16, 1931, at a cost of $846,000. Drivers paid a 35¢ toll until the structure was paid off in 1953. The bridge enabled Route 1 to continue along the coast; the old section of Route 1 via Bangor became US Route 1A. The Penobscot Narrows bridge replaced the Waldo-Hancock Bridge in 2006 after a routine inspection revealed significant deterioration in the historic span. (Photograph by Jet Lowe, courtesy of LOC, HAER, ME, 5-BUCK.V, 1–3.)

Built in 1926, the Arcade was an entertainment complex along Route 1 in East Machias. The popular destination had a 500-seat theater, an ice-cream parlor, and a dining room. A nearby boardinghouse rented rooms for $1 a night. This photograph shows the Arcade in 1927 before it burned down. (Courtesy of PMM, LB2007.1.100604.)

Five years after a fire devastated downtown Ellsworth, city officials built a new commercial block to spur economic recovery. Known as The Grand, the project included a 730-seat movie theater and several storefronts. Boston architects Krokyn and Browne designed the 1938 Art Deco theater, which incorporated elements of stainless steel and Vitrolite glass. Today, The Grand operates as a nonprofit performing arts center. (Photograph by the author.)

THE TRIANGLE FILLING STATION ELLSWORTH, MAINE

Affluent tourists known as "rusticators" began flocking to Bar Harbor and Mount Desert Island in the 1800s, first by steamboat and eventually by automobile. The Triangle Filling Station, at the intersection of Routes 1 and 3 in Ellsworth, was perfectly located to serve wealthy visitors driving to Bar Harbor and points north. Travelers could relax in the adjacent tearoom while an attendant fueled their car. A 1931 advertisement boasted, "Greasing and Alemiting a specialty." The ad further described the hospitality awaiting motorists: "Luncheons, dinners or afternoon tea, served in attractive interior salon or spacious verandas." The "unexcelled" cuisine included steak, lobster, and chicken. The Roosevelts were said to stop here en route to their retreat on Campobello Island in New Brunswick. (Courtesy of PMM, LB2007.1.100639.)

Four

MID-COAST

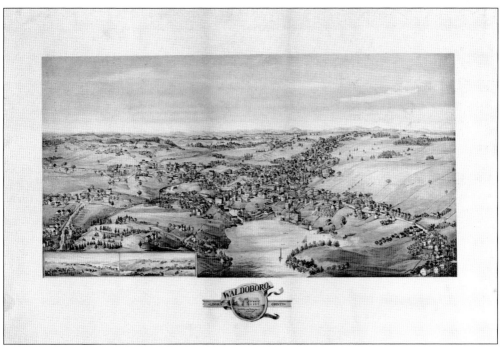

Mid-Coast Maine stretches from Brunswick to Searsport. Known for lobster shacks and lighthouses, the region also has some offbeat attractions. The movie *Peyton Place* was filmed in Camden, celebrity harbor seal Andre made his summer home in Rockport, and a store in Belfast has an albatross on display. (Courtesy of Leventhal/BPL.)

In the early days of auto travel, tourist courts were a comfortable and affordable choice for families on the move. The cozy cabins usually had two beds, a bathroom, a screened porch, and sometimes a kitchenette. Tourist courts often drew their evocative names from nature and history, with examples like Bob-O-Link, Thistle, Colonial Gables, and Ye Olde Forte. The more straightforwardly named Tourists Inn, shown here, was located on Route 1 in Searsport. (Courtesy of PMM, LB2008.19.114942.)

Fred and Florence Bastian operated the Mooring Camp Ground and Restaurant in Belfast. From 1945 to 1977, travelers arrived with their trailers and tents for a waterfront vacation. Novelist Clinton Twiss wrote about the camp in *The Long, Long Trailer*. "Here was our spot," he wrote. "Twelve acres of gently undulating lawn shaded by giant oaks." Today, those 12 acres are known as Moorings Oceanfront RV Resort. (Courtesy of PMM, LB2007.1.109542.)

The Ducktrap Bridge solved an engineering problem. The bridge was originally built in 1919 to span the Ducktrap River in Lincolnville. A second bridge was built on top of the original in 1932 to accommodate a highway grade change. The new bridge resembled a Roman aqueduct; the Historic American Engineering Record called it "one of the most unusual engineering monuments in the state." The two-tier bridge was replaced in 1999. (Courtesy of LOC, HABS, HAER ME, 14-LINC, 2-.)

The Whaleback Shell Midden, named for its size and shape, was an enormous mound of discarded oyster shells and related debris left by Native Americans along the Damariscotta River more than 1,000 years ago. European settlers began mining the midden in the late 17th century, using the shells for lime, fertilizer, road fill, and chicken feed. Today, the remains of the Whaleback Shell Midden are a state historic site. (Courtesy of PMM, LB2007.1.105159.)

The alewife is a type of herring that migrates from the ocean to spawn in freshwater lakes. The fish are used primarily for lobster bait, but they are making a comeback in the kitchen. The towns of Newcastle and Nobleboro have harvested alewives since the 1700s, and Damariscotta Mills is home to a historic fish ladder that supports the trip to fresh water. The towns built the ladder in 1807 at the request of the state (Maine was part of Massachusetts then) after a sawmill blocked access to the freshwater falls between the Damariscotta River and Damariscotta Lake. After 200 years of use, the fish ladder fell into disrepair, and a 10-year restoration project was completed in 2017. The Alewife Festival celebrates the harvest; shown here are contestants for the title of Alewife Queen in 1957. (Courtesy of Maine Department of Sea and Shore Fisheries.)

Poultry was big business in Waldo County, and Maine Broiler Day was established in 1948 for industry leaders to get together in Belfast. With chicken as king, Belfast needed a queen. Enter Betty Perry, who was named the first Broiler Queen in 1949; here she is, receiving her crown from Maine governor Frederick G. Payne. (Courtesy of Belfast Historical Society and Museum.)

Broiler Day gradually evolved from a trade meeting to a community event known as the Maine Broiler Festival. In 1957, the festival attracted 14,000 visitors who ate more than 11 tons of barbecued chicken. After the area's two major poultry plants closed in the 1980s, the broiler festival was renamed the Bay Festival. (Courtesy of Belfast Historical Society and Museum.)

The Colonial Theatre is easy to spot in downtown Belfast. Just look for the elephant on the roof. The theater opened in 1912, burned down in 1923, and reopened a year later. The current stucco façade was part of a 1947 renovation, and the rooftop elephant (named Hawthorne) came from Perry's Nut House 50 years later. Here, the theater is screening *Scandal for Sale*, which was released in 1932, well before Hawthorne showed up. (Courtesy of Belfast Historical Society and Museum.)

Erskine York began working as Yorkie the Clown in 1926. The Rockland native performed with Ringling Brothers and Barnum & Bailey Circus, among others, before leaving the big top in 1933. Settling in Camden, he ran a hot dog stand for a while and opened Yorkies Diner in 1944. York sold the diner around 1958 and continued to make local appearances in his clown getup. When he died in 1966, the businesses on Camden's Main Street closed for a half hour in his honor. (Courtesy of PMM, LB2007.1.106459.)

In June 1957, Twentieth Century Fox began filming *Peyton Place*. Most of the shooting took place in Camden, but the movie also used locations in Belfast, Rockland, Lincolnville, Rockport, and Thomaston to stand in for the small-town New Hampshire setting of the Grace Metalious book. The greeting on the Camden-Rockport Archway was transformed into "Welcome to Peyton Place," and hundreds of locals earned $10 a day as extras in the film's crowd scenes. The movie premiered on December 11, 1957, at the Camden Theater. The bestselling volume with its depictions of sex and violence was once considered so scandalous that towns in New Hampshire and Vermont turned away the filmmakers, and the Camden Public Library did not have a copy in its collection. Today, the library embraces the melodramatic film and hosted a *Peyton Place* retrospective in 2016. (Courtesy of Camden Public Library, Walsh History Center.)

Bertha (left) and Percy Moody opened three tourist cabins in Waldoboro in 1927, charging $1 a night. They soon added a lunch wagon. The wagon eventually became Moody's Diner, and the cabins evolved into Moody's Motel and Cabins. The Moody family still owns the property, and a fourth generation now welcomes hungry travelers with comfort food and pie—lots of pie. (Courtesy of Moody's Diner.)

Robert H. Reny, known as "R.H.," founded his namesake store in Damariscotta in October 1949. When business slowed down over that first winter, Reny loaded up his car and sold merchandise door-to-door. "He didn't sell a lot," Reny's son John said in a magazine interview. "But he drank a lot of coffee and ate a lot of pie." Come spring, Reny's new friends became his customers, and Renys is now a third-generation business with locations across Maine. (Photograph by George French, courtesy of MSA.)

Lobster fishing is one of the largest—and arguably the most visible—parts of Maine's economy. In 2021, the Maine lobster catch was 108 million pounds, worth a record-high $725 million. The industry employs about 4,000 people directly and thousands more in related businesses. (Courtesy of National Archives, 6372015.)

What goes into a Maine lobster roll? Take a split hot dog bun, buttered and grilled, and pile on the lobster meat. Some people add mayonnaise; others prefer butter. Red's Eats in Wiscasset offers both, along with generous portions of lobster. Millie and Harold "Red" Delano bought a food stand called Al's Eats in the 1950s and renamed it Red's. When Allen Gagnon bought Red's in 1977, he kept the name. Gagnon died in 2008, and today his children continue the family legacy, one lobster roll at a time. (Courtesy of Red's Eats.)

The Maine State Prison was built in 1824 in a section of Thomaston with a limestone quarry where prisoners could be put to work. The prison burned down in 1923, and a new facility was built on the site. The prison closed in 2002 and was demolished; inmates were moved to a new facility in Warren. (Courtesy of PMM, LB2007.1.102717.)

Unique among Mid-Coast's gift shops is the Maine State Prison Showroom in Thomaston, which sells goods created by inmates. The Maine Department of Corrections runs the shop at the site of the former prison. The items range from furniture to cornhole boards, and they are stamped "Hand Crafted at the Maine State Prison." (Courtesy of Maine Department of Corrections.)

Fred Cox, owner of Hallet's Drug Store, installed a Seth Thomas street clock on Front Street in Bath in 1915. In 1966, Harry Crooker acquired the clock and moved it a few doors over, where it stands today. Crooker and his family donated the clock to the city of Bath with a proviso to maintain the clock in working order, and it continues to keep time on Front Street. (Photograph by the author.)

Thomas Worcester Hyde established Bath Iron Works along the Kennebec River in 1884. The shipyard launched its first naval gunboat, USS *Machias*, in 1891. For the next century, Bath Iron Works built gunboats, yachts, freighters, and fishing trawlers. At its peak during World War II, the shipyard launched a destroyer every 17 days. Shown here are the USS *John L. Hall* (left) and USS *Audrey Fitch*. (Courtesy of National Archives, 394307.)

In 1896, the residents of Camden voted to establish a free public library. After years of planning and fundraising, the Camden Public Library opened in 1928. Philanthropist Mary Louise Curtis Bok donated the land, and architects Parker Morse Hooper and Charles Greely Loring designed the structure. In 1931, Bok gave additional land to the library and hired landscape architect Fletcher Steele to create a public amphitheater. (Courtesy of Camden Public Library, Walsh History Center.)

Harriet Beecher Stowe and her family moved to a house in Brunswick in 1850 when her husband, Calvin, accepted a professorship at Bowdoin College. During her two years in Brunswick, she wrote the influential novel *Uncle Tom's Cabin*. Today, Bowdoin College uses the house for faculty offices; Harriet's Writing Room is a public space within the structure commemorating Stowe's literary legacy. (Photograph by George French, courtesy of MSA.)

Princess Watahwaso was the stage name for Lucy Nicolar, who was a Penobscot performer and activist born on the Indian Island reservation in 1882. Nicolar was a mezzo-soprano who recorded with Victor Records. She married Bruce Poolaw from the Kiowa Tribe of Oklahoma, and they opened a gift shop on Indian Island called Chief Poolaw's TeePee in 1947. (Courtesy of PMM, LB2016.13.54.)

In 1943, First Lady Eleanor Roosevelt visited the Camden shipyard for the launch of the barge *Pine Tree*. The 194-foot wooden barge was the first in a series built to transport coal. Members of the Penobscot Nation took part in the launch ceremony and bestowed a beaded headdress on the first lady. Shown from left to right are Roosevelt, Princess Watahwaso, and Chief Bruce Poolaw. (Courtesy of Franklin D. Roosevelt Presidential Library and Museum.)

Rockport skin diver Harry Goodridge found an abandoned seal pup in 1961 and named him Andre. Goodridge raised the seal and taught him tricks before releasing him into the ocean. The seal wintered farther south but always returned to Rockport. Goodridge and Andre put on informal shows every summer, and the seal became a celebrity. Andre was found dead in 1986 at the age of 25. (Courtesy of the Goodridge family.)

Goodridge's daughter Toni Goodridge spoke about Andre: "While in the safety of his pen or at the aquariums, Andre was comical, eagerly showing off his tricks to tens of thousands of people over the years," she said. "But he could be ornery and unpredictable in the wild, refusing to get out of fishermen's dinghies or tugging on the flippers of scuba divers." A granite statue of Andre carved by Jane Wasey was dedicated at Rockport's harbor in 1978. (Photograph by the author.)

A fire leveled part of downtown Rockland in 1920, and the Strand Theater was the first new structure to emerge from the ashes. The Egyptian Revival movie palace opened in 1923 with a screening of My Wild Irish Rose. Businessman Joseph Dondis owned the theater, which stayed in his family until 2000. The Simmons family bought the Strand in 2004, and today the theater is a non-profit performing arts center. (Photograph by the author.)

The Wabanaki originally made baskets for food gathering and preparation. But when European colonists forced the tribes from their native lands, baskets became a source of economic independence and cultural survival. Beginning in the 19th century, Wabanaki weavers often set up camps to sell their wares along busy tourist roads like Route 1. Here, Penobscot basket maker and tribal advocate Florence Nicolar Shay (sister of Lucy Nicolar) works on a basket at her family's camp in Lincolnville. (Courtesy of PMM, LB2007.1.107647.)

Maine's first textile mill was built in 1809 in Brunswick on the Androscoggin River. The Cabot Manufacturing Company took over the property in 1857. At its peak, the mill employed thousands of workers, many of whom were French Canadian immigrants, and housed them in 75 tenements along Mill Street (known as "Little Canada"). In 1960, the State of Maine tore down the tenements and sent Route 1 through Little Canada. Cabot sold the mill in 1941; today, the property is a mixed-use development. (Courtesy of PMM, LB2007.1.104558.)

The Androscoggin Swinging Bridge is a pedestrian suspension bridge built in 1892 between Topsham and Brunswick. Spanning the Androscoggin River, the bridge was built for workers at Cabot Mill commuting from Topsham. John A. Roebling's Sons Company, known best for the Brooklyn Bridge, constructed the Swinging Bridge. The span has been rebuilt multiple times, and today only the wire cables are original. (Courtesy of the Pejepscot History Center.)

The Bay Point Hotel was built in 1890 on Jameson's Point in Rockland. The luxurious resort attracted affluent summer visitors who arrived by steamboat and railroad to escape the city heat. The Ricker family purchased the hotel in 1902 and renamed it the Sam-O-Set. The Maine Central Railroad bought it a few years later to promote tourism. The Samoset (as it was eventually spelled) burned down in 1972. Here, guests play croquet on the hotel's west lawn. (Courtesy of PMM, LB2007.1.102217.)

The more modestly appointed Hotel Rockland catered to business travelers and road trippers. The hotel was built in 1870 as the Lynde Hotel and became the Hotel Rockland around 1917. Located on Route 1 in downtown Rockland, the 75-room hotel claimed to have the "most beautiful cocktail lounge on the coast of Maine." The hotel burned down in 1952. (Courtesy of PMM, LB2007.1.102209.)

Irving L. Perry began selling pecans in his shop in Belfast in 1927. Soon, Perry's Nut House stocked delicacies like Brazil nuts straight from South America and coconuts still in their husks. But Perry also had a gift for self-promotion, and filled the shop with exotica like alligator hides, funhouse mirrors, and a taxidermied water buffalo shot by Pres. Theodore Roosevelt. Another Roosevelt—Eleanor—liked to stop at Perry's while driving to Campobello Island. Joshua Treat III bought the store after Perry's death in 1940 and continued the tradition. He added an albatross, a "man-eating clam," and a gorilla to the displays. Treat sold the business in 1974, and the store closed in 1997. Most of the collection was auctioned off, including an elephant dubbed Hawthorne that now sits on top of the Colonial Theatre in Belfast. When the shop reopened in 2004, the new owners managed to retrieve some of the sold-off menagerie. (Courtesy of PMM, LB2007.1.100221.)

Five

GREATER PORTLAND

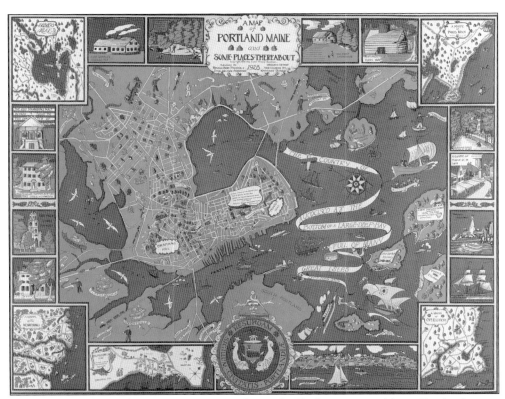

Greater Portland extends from Freeport to Scarborough. The largest city in Maine, Portland sits on a peninsula in Casco Bay and is still a working seaport. Freeport is known for a geological curiosity called the Desert of Maine, Portland saw a rum riot, and Scarborough was once home to a clam cannery with a surprising Broadway connection. (Courtesy of Leventhal/BPL.)

Once the largest hotel in New England, the Eastland is still open for business in Maine. Developer Henry P. Rines opened the hotel in 1927; he was also the man behind the Danish Village in Scarborough. The Eastland changed names and owners over the years and today is known as the Westin Portland Harborview. Shown here is the hotel when it was called the Eastland Motor Hotel, probably in the early 1960s. (Author's collection.)

The Eastland garnered some bad press in 1946 when Eleanor Roosevelt chose to leave rather than kennel her dog Fala in the garage. Instead, she and Fala found accommodation at the Royal River Cabins in Yarmouth, where they spent "a very comfortable night," per the former first lady's newspaper column. (Courtesy of Yarmouth Historical Society.)

The Danish Village brought a little piece of Europe to Scarborough in 1929. The brainchild of Portland hotelier Henry Rines and Boston architect Peter Holdensen, the themed complex had 100 individual stucco cottages modeled after the Danish town of Ribe. Costumed employees completed the European fantasy. After several ownership changes, fires, and other indignities, the village was demolished in 1976. (Courtesy of Tichnor/BPL.)

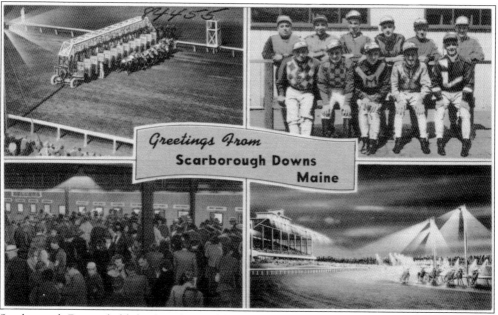

Scarborough Downs held the first thoroughbred horse race in Maine history on July 1, 1950. The state-of-the-art track had seating for 6,500 fans, stables for 1,000 horses, and parking for 6,000 cars. A few weeks after opening, Scarborough Downs installed lights and became the first thoroughbred track in the nation to offer night racing. The track switched to harness racing in the 1970s and closed for good in 2020. (Courtesy of Tichnor/BPL.)

Twin brothers Julian and Bill Leslie opened the Casco Bay Trading Post in 1947 in South Freeport. Some 20 years later, Julian saw the "Captain Brown" statue—a 25-foot-tall fiberglass fisherman—in Boothbay Harbor. Inspiration struck, and he commissioned artist Rodman Shutt to create a larger-than-life figure for the trading post. The 30-foot statue was installed in August 1969. Known officially as Chief Passamaquoddy, the statue has recently sparked controversy because of its perceived cultural insensitivity. The trading post closed in 1989. (Author's collection.)

Ernest Marstaller established the Maine Idyll Motor Court in Freeport in the 1930s, and a neon sign still beckons travelers to 20 cozy cottages. Each cottage is different, including one said to have been created from a single Maine pine tree (shown here). Today, a fourth generation of the Marstaller family runs the Maine Idyll. (Author's collection.)

CABIN BUILT FROM ONE MAINE PINE
AT THE MAINE IDYLL — FREEPORT, MAINE

Sofokli Anton, known as "Mike," opened the State O' Maine bowling center on Route 1 in Scarborough in 1950. Three types of bowling were available at first—candlepins, duckpins, and tenpins—but Big 20, as it became known, soon converted to an all-candlepin house. Anton's son Chris, who was a champion bowler, took over the business from his father and ran Big 20 for about 30 years. Today, Mike Walker owns and operates the bowling center. (Photograph by Elizabeth Budington.)

Fred H. Snow founded the eponymous F.H. Snow Canning Company in 1921 in Scarborough. At its peak, Snow's employed thousands of locals, many of whom worked out of their homes shucking clams. Snow's also had a musical theater connection. Fred Snow's grandfather Capt. Enoch Snow inspired "(When I Marry) Mister Snow," a song in the Rodgers and Hammerstein musical *Carousel*. (Courtesy of Maine Department of Marine Resources.)

Portland built its first town hall in 1825 in Market Square, a few years before it became a city. A new city hall was built on Congress Street in 1862, and the old building was razed in 1888 to make way for the Soldiers and Sailors Monument in what became Monument Square. The new city hall burned down in 1866, and its replacement burned in 1908. The current structure was built in 1908 and is still standing. (Courtesy of LOC, LC-DIG-det-4a24259.)

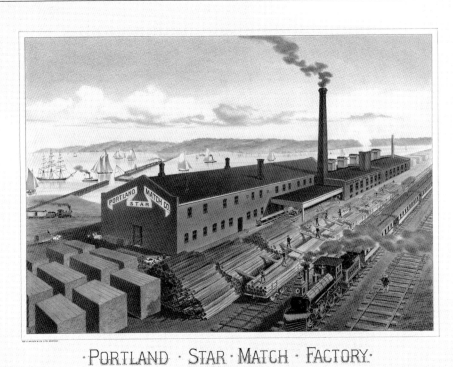

·PORTLAND · STAR · MATCH · FACTORY·
PORTLAND, ME.

The Portland Star Match Company did business in the city from 1870 to 1908. Dozens of women worked in the factory, wrapping the matches for sale and shipping. The work was dangerous—wet sponges were on hand to douse accidental fires—and the women risked phosphorus poisoning. Diamond Match Company bought the operation in 1908 and moved it out of Portland. Today the building houses commercial tenants. (Lithograph by Geo. H. Walker & Co., courtesy of LOC, LC-DIG-pga-04222.)

In 1851, newly elected Portland mayor Neal Dow (the "Napoleon of Temperance") helped enact a statewide ban on the manufacture and sale of liquor. The law was repealed in 1856, a year after the Portland Rum Riot—a violent protest fueled by information that Dow was storing liquor in city hall, supposedly for medicinal purposes. But the reprieve was brief. Restrictions were soon reimposed and stayed in effect until national prohibition was repealed in 1934. (Lithograph by E.C. Kellogg, courtesy of Special Collections, Raymond H. Fogler Library, University of Maine.)

The Portland Soldiers and Sailors Monument stands in Monument Square to honor Maine service members who were killed in the Civil War. The bronze statue, also known as Our Lady of Victories, was dedicated in 1891 and depicts a female figure holding a sword and shield. Franklin Simmons cast the bronze statue, and Richard Morris Hunt created the granite pedestal. Hunt also designed the base for the Statue of Liberty. (Courtesy of LOC, LC-DIG-det-4a08000.)

Portland's Union Station opened on St. John Street in 1888 and served three railroads: Maine Central, Boston & Maine, and Portland & Ogdensburg. The granite building had a 188-foot clock tower and was designed by Boston-based architects Bradlee, Winslow, and Wetherell. The station closed in 1960 and was demolished in 1961. The destruction of the grand station sparked a preservation movement in Portland. (Courtesy of LOC, LC-DIG-det-4a23196.)

A bronze statue honors 19th-century poet and Portland native Henry Wadsworth Longfellow. Sculptor Franklin Simmons created the likeness, and Francis H. Fassett designed the pedestal. The memorial was dedicated in 1888 at the corner of State and Congress Streets in Portland, an area now known as Longfellow Square. (Courtesy of Leslie Jones Collection, Boston Public Library.)

George Burnham and Charles Morrill founded the Burnham & Morrill Company (B&M) in 1867. B&M built a four-story cannery on Casco Bay in 1913 and began selling its well-known baked beans in 1927. B&M closed the factory in 2021 after more than a century on the Portland waterfront and sold the building to the Roux Institute at Northeastern University for development. (Photograph by George French, courtesy of MSA.)

Built in 1807 by sea captain Lemuel Moody, the Portland Observatory was a communications station for Portland's harbor. Merchants paid Moody $5 a year to receive alerts when their ships were arriving. Moody used a telescope at the top of the tower to identify vessels entering Casco Bay; he arranged flags and colored balls to notify subscribers. The observatory closed in 1923 when radios made Moody's system obsolete. It has been restored and is open to visitors. (Courtesy of LOC, HABS, ME,3-PORT,7-.)

Porteous, Mitchell and Braun opened its doors on Congress Street in downtown Portland in 1904. It was the largest department store based in Maine and well known for its elaborate Christmas displays (as seen here around 1912). After Porteous closed in the early 1990s, the Maine College of Art bought the five-story building and restored many of its historic features. In 2009, the Miller Building, which housed the store, was designated a landmark building in the Congress Street Historic District. Arthur Henri Benoit opened a men's clothing store in Westbrook in 1890. After buying out his partner C.W. Webber, Benoit opened additional stores in Portland, Lewiston, Brunswick, Biddeford, and Ogunquit. A.H. Benoit & Co. was once the largest men's clothing store in Maine and called itself "outfitters to men and boys." The last Benoit's closed in the 1990s. (Courtesy of Collections of the Maine Historical Society.)

Leon Leonwood Bean returned from a 1911 hunting trip with wet feet and a new idea. He created a boot that combined rubber bottoms with leather uppers. Bean began selling his (now famous) Maine hunting shoe by direct mail in 1912, but things did not go smoothly at first. Ninety of the first 100 sold were returned because the leather separated from the rubber. (Courtesy of PMM, LB2010.9.119259.)

Bean soon got the shoes right and opened the first L.L. Bean store on Main Street in Freeport. In 1951, the store began to stay open around the clock to better serve its customers. "We have thrown away the key to the place," Bean famously said. Today, a giant (size 410) hunting boot stands outside the flagship location and the Bootmobile is parked nearby. (Author's collection.)

At the turn of the 20th century, streetcar companies expanded their markets by building so-called trolley parks at the end of their lines and then shuttling tourists to these new destinations. The Portland Railroad Company opened Riverton Trolley Park in 1896, and people paid a nickel to ride the rails from Portland's Monument Square. Riverton Park enticed visitors with boat rides on the Presumpscot River, a petting zoo, vaudeville performances, an amusement casino, and walking paths. Here, visitors watch a performance at the Rustic Theater. Riverton closed in 1929 and became a Portland city park in 1947. Today, the Portland Parks Conservancy and the city are working to revitalize the park. (Courtesy of LOC, LC-DIG-det-4a19620.)

Brunswick, Maine., Merrymeeting Park Casino.

Amos Fitz Gerald was known as the Electric Railway King. In 1886, he invested in electric power plants in Fairfield and Waterville, and began to add electric trolley companies and destination trolley parks to his portfolio. His equation was simple: Trolley parks attracted people, people rode trolleys, and trolleys used electricity. (Author's collection.)

The Old Tower, South Freeport, Maine

Gerald opened Merrymeeting Park in Brunswick in 1898; Casco Castle in South Freeport followed in 1903. The elaborate properties offered lodging and entertainment, and each had a zoo. Merrymeeting Park closed in 1906 after patronage dropped off. A fire destroyed Casco Castle in 1914, but the stone tower survived and is still visible today. After Gerald died in 1913, electric trolley cars across the state stopped for three minutes as a sign of respect. (Courtesy of Tichnor/BPL.)

"TOONA" AT THE DESERT OF MAINE

Is it a curiosity or a cautionary tale? Either way, the Desert of Maine is like nothing else in New England. A few miles off Route 1 in Freeport, the so-called desert was first created when glaciers deposited sandy silt across southern Maine. Topsoil gradually covered the sand, making it suitable for agriculture, and a farmer named William Tuttle began working 300 acres in the late 1700s. Unfortunately, future Tuttles made some bad decisions—they failed to rotate crops and allowed sheep to overgraze—and the sand began to emerge. The Tuttles abandoned their property after the sand buried 40 acres, and Henry Goldrup bought the land in 1919. Goldrup set his sights on Route 1 travelers and rebranded the sandy spot as a tourist attraction in 1925, complete with live camels. Today, the camels are fiberglass, and the Desert of Maine offers tours, trails, and family-friendly activities. (Author's collection.)

Six

MAINE BEACHES

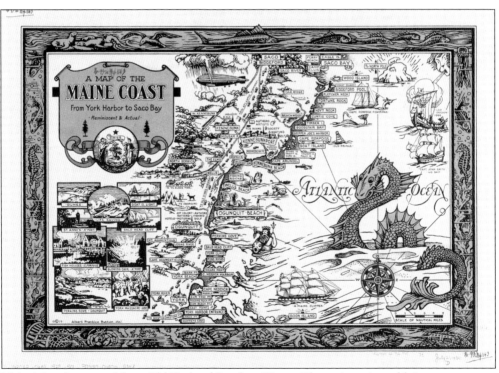

Maine's beaches extend from Old Orchard Beach to Kittery. The region mixes old-time amusements like roller coasters and drive-in theaters with reminders of the state's textile manufacturing legacy. Ogunquit has two historic theaters, Wells had a neon duck, and an image of the Nubble Lighthouse was launched into outer space. (Courtesy of Leventhal/BPL.)

Separated by the Saco River, Biddeford and Saco share a history of textile manufacturing. The Saco Manufacturing Company built a seven-story cotton mill on Indian Island (later known as Cutts Island, Factory Island, and Saco Island) in 1826. After a fire destroyed the structure in 1830, the York Manufacturing Company built a new cotton mill on the burned-out foundation. As York prospered and expanded on the island, Laconia Mills and Pepperell Mills (shown here) were established in Biddeford. The combined mill district was one of the largest in the country and employed as many as 9,000 workers. After the textile mills closed, many of the buildings were converted to industrial and residential uses, and the Biddeford–Saco Mills Historic District was listed in the National Register of Historic Places in 2008. (Photograph by George French, courtesy of MSA.)

When Charles Tufts opened the Drakes Island Motel in 1958, he installed a neon sign in the shape of a male duck, or drake. Tufts's granddaughter Tracy Elkins remembered the drake in its glory days. "He was a beauty!" she told the *York County Coast Star*. "When we were kids, we couldn't wait for it to be dark so my papa would turn the lights on." When Paul (Charles's son) and Pat Tufts sold the Wells motel in 2013, they kept the sign. (Photograph by Robert Cadloff.)

John M. Davis built the Island Ledge Casino in Wells Beach around 1909. The venue housed a dance hall, ice-cream parlor, movie theater, bowling alley, pool room, and dining room. Typical of the early days of the game, the bowling alley had wall-mounted scorepads and appeared to have balls for both candlepins and tenpins. (Courtesy of PMM, LB2008.19.116845.)

After his successful 1927 flight across the Atlantic Ocean, Charles A. Lindbergh and the *Spirit of St. Louis* embarked on a goodwill tour that covered 48 states in three months. En route from New Hampshire to Maine, Lindbergh encountered fog at the Scarborough airport and landed instead in Old Orchard Beach on July 24, 1927. Lindbergh and his plane are shown here at an unidentified location. (Photograph by Harris & Ewing, courtesy of LOC, LC-DIG-hec-34667.)

The Biddeford & Saco Railroad began service on July 4, 1888, with horse cars running between Biddeford and Old Orchard Beach. Efforts to electrify the line began in 1890, and the first electric trolleys ran in 1892. The railway operated until 1939, when buses replaced electric cars, and the last trolley ran on July 5, 1939. (Photograph by Charles Brown, courtesy of Seashore Trolley Museum.)

Lindbergh's crossing inspired others to duplicate the feat. French millionaire Armand Lotti was among them. Blinded in one eye from a hunting accident, Lotti hired aviators Jean Assollant and René Lefèvre to accompany him in the *Oiseau Canari*. Dubbed "Yellow Bird," the plane took off from Old Orchard Beach (a slight detour from Route 1) on June 13, 1929. The tail dragged a bit on takeoff, and the reason soon became clear. Stowaway Arthur Schreiber surprised the crew 20 minutes into the flight. "For a moment we wanted to throw him overboard," Lotti later told the *New York Times*. They chose leniency instead, and the plane managed an emergency landing in Spain. The crew eventually made a triumphant appearance in Paris, and the Yellow Bird is still on display at Paris–Le Bourget Airport. (Courtesy of Leslie Jones Collection, Boston Public Library.)

Alcide Cote opened the Vacationland Motor Court on Route 1 in Saco. His granddaughter Celeste Nadeau Baranyi remembers growing up there. She would play shuffleboard with the guests, many of whom returned year after year. "It was like having a dozen grandparents," she recalled. Claire and Bert Dube purchased the motor court in 1977 and hoped to build a candlepin bowling alley on the site. When the city would not extend sewer lines to the property, they found another parcel on Route 1 and opened Vacationland Bowling and Recreation Center in 1983. What was the best part of running a bowling center? Claire Dube was quick to answer: "It was meeting so many wonderful people." Vacationland introduced computerized scoring to the candlepin game, an innovation that scandalized traditionalists at the time. The Dubes sold the motor court in 2002 and closed the bowling center in 2017. (Courtesy of Andrew F. Wood and Jenny L. Wood.)

The story of Funtown Splashtown USA began in 1960 when Violet (left) and Ken Cormier opened the Marvel Drive-in restaurant on Route 1 in Saco. They added some rides, and Funtown USA was born. Attractions included bumper cars, a merry-go-round, and something called the Luv Machine. The Galaxi roller coaster arrived in 1978. Manufactured by a now-defunct Italian company, the Galaxi was the first roller coaster in Maine. (Palace Playland in Old Orchard Beach installed its own Galaxi in 1994.) In the 1990s, the Cormiers added a water park and named the combined attraction Funtown Splashtown USA. They introduced the Excalibur roller coaster in 1998, a wooden model designed to add a dose of nostalgia to the thrills. Ken died in 2013, but the park remains in the family, and Violet is still actively involved in daily operations. (Courtesy of Funtown Splashtown USA.)

The Saco Drive In was the first drive-in theater built in Maine. It opened on July 15, 1939, as the Motor-In Theatre and showed *Forbidden Music* (originally titled *Land without Music*). When the owners sold the property in 2022, the theater moved across Route 1 to a new home at the Aquaboggan Water Park. (Photograph by the author.)

A lighthouse in space? Not exactly. But a photo of Cape Neddick Light Station was included among the 116 digitized images carried on the Voyager spacecraft to explain life on earth to extraterrestrials. Completed in 1879, the lighthouse is better known as Nubble Light because it was built on a "nub" of land off the Cape Neddick section of York. (Photograph by Richard Cheek, courtesy of LOC, HABS ME, 16-YOR, 3-.)

It is easy to imagine mid-century travelers making the short detour from Route 1 to spend a night at the Starlite Motel in Old Orchard Beach. Its neon sign was one of multiple "diving lady" signs across the country, meant to conjure up visions of a refreshing dip in the motel's pool after a long day on the road. (Photograph by John Margolies, courtesy of LOC, LC-MA05-8543.)

An important piece of Black history is just a short detour off Route 1 in Kittery. Hazel and Clayton Sinclair ran Rock Rest, a guest house that welcomed Black travelers, from the 1940s through the 1970s. Although Maine did not have formal Jim Crow segregation laws, Black travelers routinely met with discrimination during that era. Rock Rest fell into disrepair after the Sinclairs died but was recently restored and listed in the National Register of Historic Places and the Black Heritage Trail of New Hampshire. (Photograph by the author.)

The Palace Diner has been serving meals to hungry customers in Biddeford since 1927. The 15-seat diner (no tables or booths) was built by the Pollard Company in Lowell, Massachusetts, and is one of only two remaining lunch cars from this manufacturer. The Riverside Diner in Bristol, New Hampshire, is the other survivor. (Photograph by the author.)

After retiring from the restaurant business in Boston in the 1940s, Socrates "Louie" Toton opened the Maine Restaurant in Wells. Toton spent summers in his garden and opened the restaurant only in the winter months. Brothers Myles and Dick Henry bought the place in 1983 and renamed it the Maine Diner. Jim MacNeill became the third owner of the diner in 2018 after serving as general manager for 14 years. And, yes, Toton's garden is still supplying fresh produce. (Photograph by Mark H. Stein.)

Edward and Mattie Talpey opened the Goldenrod across from Short Sands Beach in 1896. The York Beach spot quickly became famous for its salt-water taffy, dubbed "Goldenrod Kisses," which Edward pulled by hand in the shop's front window. Although taffy pulling is now mechanized, the Goldenrod still makes those kisses—about eight million pieces of taffy a year—and people continue to line up at the windows to watch. (Photograph by the author.)

The electric street railway came to York Beach in 1897, establishing the waterfront community as a tourist destination. The Fun-O-Rama arcade offers classic boardwalk games such as Skee-Ball, and six candlepin bowling lanes are next door. No bowling shoes are required, and keeping score is strictly a paper-and-pencil affair. York's Wild Kingdom, which bills itself as New England's only zoo and amusement park, is down the street. (Photograph by the author.)

In 1944, William Hancock bought the Ogunquit Lobster Pound (which dated from 1931) as a gift for his wife, Hazel. When William died a year later, Hazel ran the business with the help of her three sisters and kept the restaurant going until 1967, when Hazel's son William Jr. and his wife, Alma, took over. Current owner Bill Hancock bought out his parents in 1984 and still carries on the family tradition. (Courtesy of PMM, LB2007.20.119834.)

After a fire damaged his Kennebunk home in 1852, George Washington Bourne rebuilt the barn and carriage house in the Carpenter Gothic style and embellished the main house to match the updated outbuildings. Dubbed the "Wedding Cake House," the ornate home is sometimes called "the most photographed house in Maine." (Photograph by George French, courtesy of MSA.)

Ogunquit has attracted artists since the 1890s. Charles Woodbury began offering summer classes in 1898 at his Ogunquit School of Drawing and Painting. A few years later, Hamilton Easter Field settled in Ogunquit and established the Summer School of Graphic Arts. Together, these influential artists helped establish Ogunquit as an artist colony. (Photograph by George French, courtesy of MSA.)

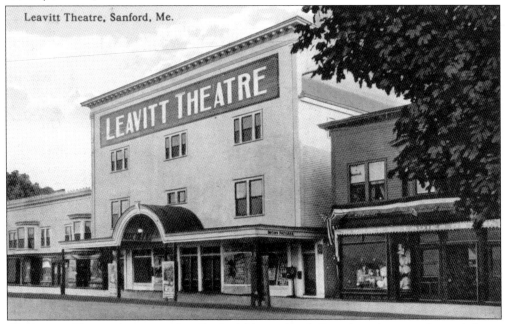

The Leavitt Theatre first opened in Sanford (shown here). But when the venue burned down, Frank and Annie Leavitt regrouped and opened the Leavitt Fine Arts Theatre in Ogunquit. The new cinema debuted in 1924 and showed first-run and art films every summer for decades. Peter Clayton bought the Leavitt in 1976 and continued the tradition. When it was time to invest in digital projection equipment, Clayton found community support through a crowdfunding campaign in 2013. (Author's collection.)

In 1933, Broadway producer Walter Hartwig opened a summer theater in a garage in Ogunquit. The Ogunquit Playhouse attracted stars from stage and screen, and the thriving theater moved to its current location on Route 1 in 1937. After Hartwig died in 1941, his widow, Maude, took over and kept the theater afloat during the war years. She sold the venue in 1950, and the playhouse remained successful for decades. As attendance began to decline in the 1990s, the Ogunquit Playhouse Foundation was formed to preserve the theater's legacy. With the move to nonprofit ownership, the theater transitioned to an all-musical format, expanded to a 26-week season, and began to produce a holiday show for the Music Hall in Portsmouth. (Courtesy of Ogunquit Playhouse.)

Seven

NEW HAMPSHIRE

New Hampshire claims just a small piece of Route 1, which enters in Portsmouth and leaves in Seabrook. Portsmouth gives its name to the country's oldest continuously operating shipyard and is home to a decommissioned research submarine. Wealthy vacationers enjoyed the sea breezes on the Isles of Shoals, while the masses rode the electric trolley to Hampton Beach. (Courtesy of Leventhal/BPL.)

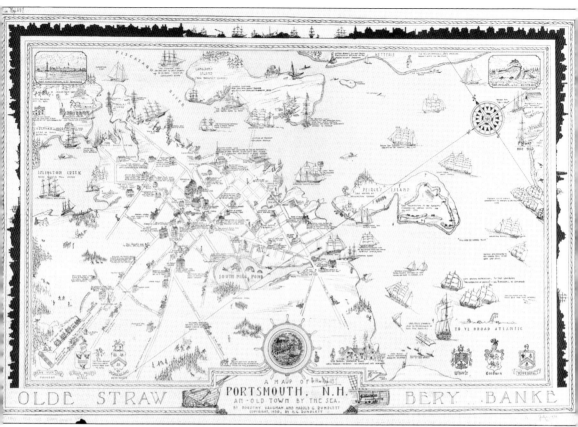

How long is New Hampshire's coastline? It depends on who is measuring. The state Department of Environmental Services lists the official figure as 18.57 miles, but NOAA defines it as only 13 miles. Route 1, which runs a bit inland, is 17 miles long. But while the Granite State's sliver of the Atlantic coast and Route 1 is tiny compared to its neighbors, access to the Piscataqua River and Atlantic Ocean had great commercial, historic, and strategic value. In 1740, King George II of England established the boundary between Maine and New Hampshire as the middle of the Piscataqua River. New Hampshire officials were not happy with this watery definition, however, and sought to extend the border to the Maine shoreline. *New Hampshire v. Maine* ended up in the US Supreme Court, which upheld the royal decree in 2001. (Courtesy of Leventhal Collection/BPL.)

The Clamshell Alliance was a grassroots organization formed in 1976 to protest the construction of the Seabrook Nuclear Power Plant. On May 1, 1977, the alliance staged a civil disobedience action; more than 2,000 protesters occupied the nuclear plant construction site, and 1,414 were arrested. In 1978, internal disagreements led to a split within the Clamshell Alliance, and a successor organization dissolved in 1981. Although a nuclear reactor was eventually built at Seabrook in 1986, citizen actions had an impact. Plans for a second reactor were scuttled, and major stockholder Public Service Company of New Hampshire declared bankruptcy in 1988. Today, NextEra Energy Resources owns and operates Seabrook Station. (Photograph by Peter Simon, courtesy of Peter Simon Collection, Robert S. Cox Special Collections and University Archives Research Center, UMass Amherst Libraries.)

The Music Hall opened in 1878 as a vaudeville theater in downtown Portsmouth. Politician, brewer, and tycoon Frank Jones bought and renovated the theater in 1901, only to die a year later. At first the Music Hall—renamed the Portsmouth Theatre—thrived under new owner (and seven-time Portsmouth mayor) F.W. Hartford. The theater often hosted Broadway shows on national tours, and luminaries like John Philip Sousa and Mark Twain made appearances. But the aging theater could not compete with the city's new entertainment venues and was transformed into a movie house called the Civic in 1945. Hard times struck again in the 1980s, and the theater closed briefly. That was when a community group called Friends of the Music Hall stepped in to restore the theater, which is now a nonprofit center for the performing arts. (Courtesy of Portsmouth Athenaeum.)

YOKEN'S

Yoken's
"THAR SHE BLOWS!"

YOKEN'S
GOOD THINGS TO EAT

LUXURY
DINNERS
$100

THAR SHE BLOWS

U.S. Route #1, Portsmouth, N.H.

90334

In 1947, Harry Yoken opened a restaurant in Portsmouth and served "luxury dinners" for $1. By 1972, Yoken's had seating for 600 customers and served 500,000 meals a year. The restaurant closed in 2004, and the building was torn down. But a few local businesses stepped up to restore and relight the beloved "Thar She Blows" neon sign, which still glows over Route 1. (Courtesy of Tichnor/BPL.)

Howard Johnson's orange-roofed restaurants were familiar sights along the nation's roadways, and the kid-friendly menu appealed to families on the move. In the 1970s, the "Host of the Highways" had three restaurants on Route 1 in Maine: Brunswick, South Portland, and Wells. Massachusetts locations included Danvers, Lynnfield, Saugus, Dedham, Walpole, and North Attleborough. In New Hampshire, the Portsmouth Howard Johnson's (shown here) was moved in 1949 to accommodate the construction of the Portsmouth Traffic Circle. (Courtesy of Portland Athenaeum.).

The Portsmouth Naval Shipyard was established in 1800 and is the US Navy's oldest continuously operating shipyard. Despite its name, the facility is not in New Hampshire, but in Maine on Seavey's Island in the Piscataqua River. The naval yard produced its first battleship in 1814; workers built and repaired vessels for the next hundred years. The shipyard began to build submarines in the 20th century, and production ramped up during World War II, when more than 70 submarines were constructed. After the war, the Portsmouth Naval Shipyard became the US Navy's center for submarine design and development. Shown here is a 1941 view of the shipyard from the west with Route 1 in the foreground. (Courtesy of US Navy.)

The USS *Squalus*, shown here under construction at the Portsmouth Naval Shipyard in 1938, suffered a catastrophic valve failure and sank off the New Hampshire coast during a test run on May 23, 1939. Divers from the USS *Falcon* began rescue operations on May 24 and saved 33 men; 26 men perished in the accident. The *Squalus* was salvaged and decommissioned later that year; the submarine was recommissioned in 1940 as the USS *Sailfish*. (Courtesy of Bureau of Ships Collection, US National Archives.)

The USS *Albacore* was used to test propulsion and control systems. *Albacore* was built at the Portsmouth Naval Shipyard and commissioned in 1953. After almost two decades as a floating laboratory, she was decommissioned in 1972 and languished in Philadelphia for over 10 years. The vessel returned to New Hampshire in 1985 and now operates as a museum in Portsmouth. (Courtesy of Collections of Naval History and Heritage Command, US Navy.)

Two exhibits invite visitors to explore the history of Portsmouth. The Black Heritage Trail of New Hampshire promotes awareness and appreciation of African American history and culture in the state. New Hampshire's African heritage dates to 1645, when the first-known Black person arrived as a slave. Hundreds of Black men and women were living in New Hampshire by the time of the American Revolution, some free and some enslaved. In 2003, construction workers digging under Chestnut Street in Portsmouth found 13 wooden coffins. Further analysis concluded that nearly 200 freed and enslaved African people were buried at the site in the 18th century. The city closed Chestnut Street and created a memorial park known as the African Burying Ground to honor those interred there. (Photograph by the author.)

Strawbery Banke is a 10-acre campus in Portsmouth's Puddle Dock neighborhood designed to bring the past alive with historic houses and gardens, costumed role players, and demonstrations of traditional crafts. Shown here is Stoodley's Tavern, which James Stoodley built on Daniel Street in 1761 to replace a previous establishment that burned down. The tavern was home to Stoodley, his wife, two children, and two enslaved Africans. In the 1760s, Stoodley hosted auctions in the building, selling enslaved Africans, along with rum and cotton. A decade later, Stoodley's became a meeting place for revolutionaries. Even Paul Revere paid a visit in 1774. Stoodley's was moved to Hancock Street in 1966, where it serves as an educational center for Strawbery Banke. (Courtesy of LOC, LC-DIG-det-4a13760.)

The Isles of Shoals are nine islands on the border between Maine and New Hampshire. Five are part of Maine: Appledore, Cedar, Duck, Malaga, and Smuttynose. Lunging, Seavey, Star, and White Islands belong to New Hampshire. Entrepreneurs built grand hotels on some of the islands in the 1800s for summer folk seeking sea breezes and ocean views. Today, only the Oceanic Hotel on Star Island remains. The men shown here were visiting Appledore. Smuttynose Island was the site of a double murder in 1873. Maren Hontvet, her sister Karen Christensen, and their brother's wife Anethe Christensen were alone overnight on the isolated island. In what was likely a robbery gone wrong, Louis Wagner rowed to the island from Portsmouth, killed Karen and Anethe, and stole $15. Maren escaped and hid until daybreak at a spot now called "Maren's Rock." Wagner was captured in Boston and transported to Portsmouth, where a mob almost killed him. He stood trial in Maine and was convicted and hanged in 1875. (Courtesy of LOC, LC-DIG-det-4a16768.)

The World War I Memorial Bridge carried Route 1 across the Piscataqua River between New Hampshire and Maine. The vertical-lift bridge opened in 1923 and was replaced 90 years later. A plaque on the bridge honored the New Hampshire sailors and soldiers who took part in World War I. Shown here is five-year-old Eileen Foley (then known as Helen Dondero), front and center, with a group of dignitaries at the opening ceremony. Foley grew up to be an eight-term mayor of Portsmouth and, coming full circle, dedicated the replacement bridge in 2013. (Courtesy of Collections of Maine Historical Society.)

BANDSTAND HAMPTON BEACH, N. H. C155

Hampton Beach is a seaside resort along Route 1A in New Hampshire, just a few miles from US-1. In 1897, the Town of Hampton voted to lease the beach property to the newly formed Hampton Beach Improvement Company (HBIC) to transform the waterfront into a recreational center. Also that year, an electric trolley was built to bring travelers to the water; the first spike was driven at the intersection of Route 1 and Winnacunnet Road in Hampton. The trolley carried 555,000 people in its first year of operation. Around the turn of the 20th century, developer Wallace D. Lovell made a deal with HBIC to build several structures: the Hampton Beach Casino, Ocean House hotel, and an opera house and bandstand (shown here). He also built a mile-long wooden bridge between Hampton Beach and Seabrook. HBIC's 99-year lease expired in 1997; oversight returned to the town, which continues to update this enduring resort. (Courtesy of PMM, LB2007.1.31058.)

Eight

MASSACHUSETTS

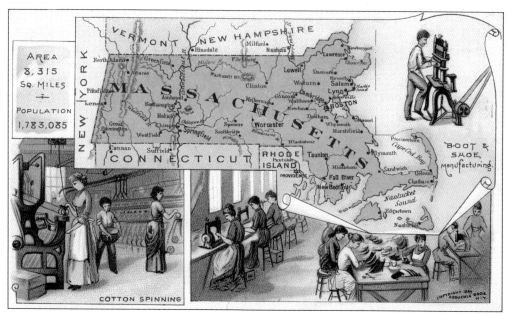

Route 1 enters Massachusetts in Salisbury and exits in Attleboro; the road follows the interstate through Boston. Dizzy Gillespie once played at a celebrated jazz club in Peabody, an orange dinosaur towered over a miniature golf course in Saugus, and a giant clown welcomed families to an amusement park in North Attleborough. (Courtesy of Leventhal/BPL.)

Owned and operated by the Galanis family, the Agawam Diner was first located in Ipswich (shown here). When the Ipswich location closed, the structure spent some time in Peabody and moved again. The third time was the charm, and the Agawam Diner has occupied the same spot on Route 1 in Rowley since 1970. Today, the Galanis family still serves diner staples like meatloaf, American chop suey, and lemon meringue pie. (Courtesy of Larry Cultrera collection.)

Fowle's News occupied a storefront on Main Street in Newburyport since 1903. Since the 1920s, half of the building's ground-floor space was used as a soda fountain and restaurant. The building has a historic neon sign advertising sodas and cigars and an Art Deco Vitrolite banner sign reading "News Store" and "Soda Shop." Several restaurants have tested in the space since the newsstand closed in 2012. (Photograph by the author.)

The Topsfield Fair traces its roots to 1818 when the Essex Agricultural Society was formed. The society held its first cattle show in 1820. After moving around Essex County for almost a century, the fair established a permanent home at the Treadwell Farm in Topsfield in 1910. Today, the fair offers livestock displays, rides and games, a pumpkin weigh-off, and the Mrs. Essex County pageant. (Courtesy of Historic New England.)

The classic Broadway Flying Horses carousel was the centerpiece of Salisbury Beach's attractions from 1913 to 1977, when it was sold. In 2019, the nonprofit Salisbury Beach Partnership sought to return a vintage carousel to the beach and purchased a 1909 Looff-Mangels carousel with 44 hand-carved and decorated wooden animals. A new pavilion will house the oceanfront carousel, ensuring year-round entertainment. (Courtesy of Salisbury Beach Partnership.)

HISTORIC HOME OF PUTNAM PANTRY CANDIES

CANDIES

U. S. ROUTE NO.1, DANVERS, MASSACHUSETTS E-12437

In 1951, Galo Putnam Emerson opened a candy shop in an old shoe factory on Route 1 in Danvers. More than 70 years later, Putnam Pantry is still owned and operated by the Emerson family. (Author's collection.)

The Emersons are direct descendants of Gen. Israel Putnam, who fought in the French and Indian War and the American Revolution. Known as "Old Put," he was a key figure at the Battle of Bunker Hill in 1775. He is popularly credited with telling the revolutionary troops, "Don't fire until you see the whites of their eyes," although some historians have questioned the story. Putnam was born in 1718 on Maple Street in Danvers (then Salem Village); the house is adjacent to the candy shop. (Photograph by Frank Cousins, courtesy of Phillips Library, Peabody Essex Museum, Frank Cousins Collection of Glass Plate Negatives, Box 6_175.)

A Mister Peanut sign once stood outside a Planters Peanut store on Route 1 in Peabody. When the Half Dollar Bar replaced the nut shop in the 1960s, Mister Peanut was transformed into a debonair man wearing a tuxedo. After the bar closed in the 1980s, Planters Peanuts rescued the sign, refurbished it, and placed it on display at its plant in Fort Smith, Arkansas. (Photograph by John Margolies, courtesy of LOC, LC-DIG-mrg-02334.)

Fern's Motel opened in 1952 in Saugus. The motel acquired an unsavory reputation over the years, capped by a brief police standoff in 2014. It was demolished in 2015, although the graffiti-covered plastic sign—a replacement for the original neon shown here—was still standing as of this writing. (Courtesy of Andrew F. Wood and Jenny L. Wood.)

Frank Giuffrida transformed a seedy bar called the Gyro Club into a Western-themed steakhouse in Saugus. The Hilltop Steak House opened in 1961 with a herd of fiberglass cattle and a 68-foot neon cactus. The six dining rooms evoked a New Englander's vision of the Wild West, with names like Sioux City and Santa Fe. By the 1980s, the Hilltop was the busiest restaurant in the United States, serving generous portions at low prices, and customers would happily wait over an hour for one of the restaurant's 1,400 seats. Giuffrida sold the restaurant in 1988, and the Hilltop closed in 2013. Everything was auctioned off except the sign and the cactus. Both were updated and incorporated into a new development on the site. Giuffrida died in 2003. (Photograph by the author.)

In 1958, Madeline and William Wong bought a 50-seat restaurant in Saugus. They called their new enterprise the Kowloon Restaurant and Cocktail Lounge and slowly turned the modest spot into a 1,200-seat restaurant and entertainment complex. A 30-foot tiki god greets customers, themed dining rooms have names like Volcano Bay, and performers from Jerry Seinfeld to Frankie Avalon have played the showroom. The next generation of the Wong family still operates Kowloon. (Photograph by the author.)

Weylu's had a brief but memorable run in Saugus. Restaurateurs Rick and Wilma Chang opened the 1,500-seat restaurant in 1989. Built at a cost of $13 million, Weylu's was modeled after the Forbidden City and boasted lavish details throughout. After a strong start, business slowed, debt mounted, and Weylu's closed in 1999. Several new owners tried and failed to make a go of the restaurant, and the former Weylu's was demolished in 2015. (Courtesy of Anthony Sammarco.)

In 1961, the Prince Macaroni Company owned a failing pizza place on Route 1 in Saugus. To turn the restaurant around, the company made a sweet deal with employee Arthur Castraberti: if he could make the "Leaning Tower of Pizza" successful within 10 years, it would be his. With the help of his family, Castraberti transformed the once-troubled drive-in into a thriving restaurant. Today, Castraberti's son Steven runs the 700-seat Prince Pizzeria. (Photograph by John Margolies, courtesy of LOC, LC-DIG-mrg-07218.)

Retired sea captain James F. Wilkinson opened a small refreshment stand in Lynnfield in 1925. He spent the next few years building a ship, which opened as Ships' Haven restaurant around 1930 but was eventually called the Ship Restaurant. Customers crossed a gangplank to enter the nautical-themed dining spot, which sported portholes "as authentic as those used in the construction of ocean-going liners," according to the restaurant's website. The Ship Restaurant was demolished in 2017. (Photograph by James F. Taulman, courtesy of Boston Public Library.)

The Route 1 Miniature Golf and Batting Cages are gone, but the orange dinosaur lives on. A fiberglass Tyrannosaurus rex stood guard over the family-owned business, which opened in 1958 in Saugus, staring down cars on Route 1. After second-generation owner Diana Fay sold the property in 2016, arrangements were made to incorporate the dinosaur into the new development on the site. (Photograph by the author.)

Hockeytown is an indoor hockey rink in Saugus. John Abbott opened the original Hockeytown in 1965 in a converted bus terminal in Melrose. The Saugus facility opened on Route 1 in 1972, and Abbott's son Larry began managing the center after he graduated from college in 1973. The Melrose rink closed in 1978, but the Saugus ice remained in the Abbott family until 2018. (Photograph by the author.)

Lennie's on the Turnpike was a legendary jazz club on Route 1 in Peabody. Lennie Sogoloff opened a roadhouse with a jukebox full of jazz records in the early 1950s and began booking live acts a few years later. As the club's reputation grew, everyone from Dizzy Gillespie to Buddy Rich played at Lennie's. The jazz spot burned to the ground in 1971 just a few hours after pianist Earl "Fatha" Hines played a Saturday night set. (Courtesy of Lennie's on the Turnpike Collection, Salem State University Archives and Special Collections.)

Karl and Regina Engel opened Karl's Sausage Kitchen in Saugus in 1958. Karl learned to make sausage from his father in what was then East Germany and brought the old-world recipes to Massachusetts. When Anita and Robert Gokey bought the business in 2007, they kept the name but moved the property from Route 1 to a new spot in Peabody. (Photograph by Kristen Nyberg.)

022186. LARGEST DRYDOCK IN COUNTRY, CHARLESTON NAVY YARD

COPYRIGHT 1905 BY DETROIT PUBLISHING CO.

The US Navy established the Charlestown Navy Yard in 1800; it was one of six shipyards built along the Atlantic coast from Portsmouth to Norfolk, Virginia. Also called the Boston Naval Shipyard, it sits at the junction of the Charles and Mystic Rivers in Boston's Inner Harbor. Starting with the USS *Independence* in 1814, workers built more than 200 ships and repaired countless others during the shipyard's nearly 200-year history. The navy yard's most productive years began in the 1930s; the workforce launched more than 6,000 naval ships by the end of World War II in 1945. During the war years, the yard had more than 50,000 employees and hired women and people of color for production jobs for the first time. The federal government closed the Charlestown Navy Yard in 1974; part of the facility is now a national historic site. Shown here is the USS *Maryland* in dry dock. (Courtesy of LOC, LC-DIG-det-4a15774.)

The USS *Constitution* is the oldest commissioned ship in the US Navy. Launched in 1797, she earned the nickname "Old Ironsides" in the War of 1812 after a battle with the British frigate HMS *Guerriere* when enemy cannonballs appeared to bounce off her thick oak hull. The *Constitution* was retired from active service in 1881 and designated a museum ship in 1907. Today, she is berthed in the former Charlestown Navy Yard and is open for public tours. In this photograph from around 1930, people are lined up to see the historic warship. (Courtesy of Leslie Jones Collection, Boston Public Library.)

The Battle of Bunker Hill was a bloody skirmish fought on Breed's Hill in Charlestown (not Bunker Hill) on June 17, 1775. The British claimed victory, but the encounter proved the mettle of the Revolutionary army. Fifty years later, war hero Marquis de Lafayette laid the cornerstone for the Bunker Hill monument. The 221-foot granite obelisk was a rare celebration of an American military defeat. (Courtesy of Henry Peabody Collection, National Archives, 155823637.)

John Winthrop the Younger established the Saugus Iron Works in 1646. Until then, the American colonies did not have the technology to manufacture iron, which was used in everything from weapons to horseshoes. Skilled workers were recruited from England; indentured servants from Scotland often provided unskilled labor. The ironworks closed around 1670; the facility was added to the National Park Service system almost three centuries later in 1968. (Photograph by Samuel Chamberlain, courtesy of the Samuel Chamberlain Collection of Photographic Negatives, Phillips Library, Peabody Essex Museum, Chamberlain_002393.)

The Maurice J. Tobin Memorial Bridge opened in 1950 and spans the Mystic River between the city of Chelsea and Boston's Charlestown neighborhood. The Tobin brings Route 1 into Boston, where the highway travels concurrently with Interstate 93 through the city. The bridge played a supporting role in the movie *Mystic River*, and locals remember when notorious murderer Charles Stuart jumped off the Tobin to his death in 1990. (Courtesy of Northeastern University Archives and Special Collections.)

The John F. Fitzgerald Expressway, known as the Central Artery, was an elevated highway that opened in 1950 and carried Interstate 93, US-1, and Massachusetts Route 3 through downtown Boston. The elevated roadway could not handle growing traffic, and was replaced with an underground highway as part of a complex and costly construction project nicknamed "the Big Dig." The old structure was dismantled in 2004. (Courtesy of Leslie Jones Collection, Boston Public Library.)

Roadside motels are a quintessentially American phenomenon. Usually independently owned, they beckoned travelers with elaborate neon signs and luxuries like swimming pools. Mom-and-pop motels thrived during the 1950s and 1960s, but two factors ended the golden era. National chains like Holiday Inn started to dominate the business, promising motorists an identical experience from coast to coast, and interstate highways began to divert drivers from smaller roads like Route 1. (Photograph by the author.)

Some of the remaining mom-and-pop motels found new life when tourists and preservationists rediscovered their retro charms, but many are in decline and depend heavily on budget-conscious business travelers and weekly rentals to survive. The Red Fox Motel still welcomes guests in Foxborough, and the Walpole Motel offers lodging in nearby Walpole. (Photograph by the author.)

A car dealership acquired the Arns Park Motel in North Attleborough in 2010. The family-owned motel, which dated from 1923, was torn down to make way for vehicle storage. The motel had one last hurrah before demolition, serving as a training site for local police and firefighters. (Courtesy of Andrew F. Wood and Jenny L. Wood.)

Lafayette House traces its history to 1784, when Aaron Everett established a tavern and inn along a stagecoach route in Foxborough and called it the Everett Inn. The Marquis de Lafayette reportedly spent the night at the inn in 1825 after he laid the cornerstone for the Bunker Hill Monument. George Washington and Benjamin Franklin are also said to have been guests of the establishment. (Photograph by the author.)

Motels, diners, and sweet shops lined Route 1 in Massachusetts, and advertising postcards of the time offered a glimpse into their appeal. Chisholm's Motel in Saugus offered in-room steam and whirlpool baths as well as waterbeds, while the New Englander Motor Court in Malden touted "flameless electric heat" on a promotional card. Shown here is the Avalon Motel in Saugus with its long-gone sign. (Courtesy of Larry Cultrera collection.)

Brothers Peter and William Kallas opened the Bel-Aire Diner in Peabody in the early 1950s. The Kallas family closed the diner in 2006 and sold the property. Attempts to save the eatery failed, and the historic Mountain View model diner was demolished in 2012. (Courtesy of Larry Cultrera collection.)

The Fanny Farmer Candy Fair in Peabody (shown here) was not shy about advertising its goodies. A postcard boasted the "finest foods from the world's richest markets blended into these delicious candies in our own modern kitchen for your eating pleasure." The Old Salem House in Danvers sold Connelly's Famous Candies "made from old fashioned New England recipes handed down from father to son for over half a century." (Courtesy of Larry Cultrera collection.)

Dunn's Village was a string of tourist cabins along Route 1 in Sharon. A promotional postcard boasted, "Many people tell us that we serve the finest food on the road, and it doesn't cost a fortune, either." The remodeled dining room had a fried chicken special for 75¢. In North Attleborough, the Red Rock Hill Cabins (shown here) promised basic amenities such as hot showers, radios, and a "luncheonette on premises." The name referred to a local geographic feature. (Courtesy of Tichnor/BPL.)

On April 15, 1920, a paymaster and guard were shot and killed during a robbery at a shoe company in Braintree. Italian immigrants and anarchists Nicola Sacco and Bartolomeo Vanzetti were arrested, tried, convicted, and sentenced to death. Their 1921 trial was sensationalized, and many believed the verdict reflected the anti-immigrant and anti-radical sentiments of the times. Shown here are police guarding the Norfolk County Superior Courthouse in Dedham during the trial. (Courtesy of LOC, LC-USZ62-136880.)

The Charlestown State Prison was built in 1805. Inmates incarcerated at the prison included con artist Charles Ponzi (of Ponzi scheme fame) and civil rights activist Malcolm X. On August 23, 1927, Sacco and Vanzetti were executed in the prison's electric chair. Charlestown State Prison closed in 1955; Bunker Hill Community College currently occupies the location. (Courtesy of Leslie Jones Collection, Boston Public Library.)

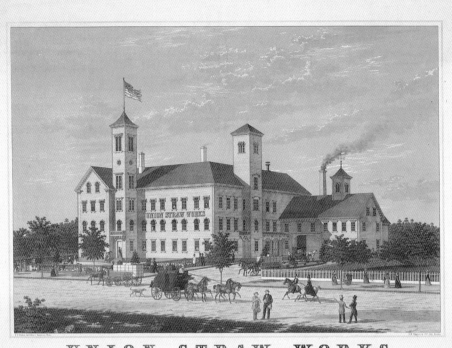

UNION STRAW WORKS.
FOXBORO MASS.
CARPENTER & C?, PROPRIETORS.

The Union Straw Works was built on Wall Street in Foxborough in 1852. Once the largest straw hat factory in the world, the enterprise employed over 6,000 workers at its peak. The factory burned to the ground in 1900 and was never rebuilt. (Courtesy of Boston Athenaeum.)

Welcoming guests on Route 1 since the 1930s, Walpole's Red Wing Diner has a secret. An unassuming clapboard building from the outside, the diner incorporates a 1930s-era Worcester Lunch Car. The dining car was the original restaurant. But as owners expanded the eatery, the lunch car's exterior was covered with siding and today serves as the restaurant's bar. Long-term employee Liam Murphy, who worked his way up from busboy to manager, purchased the diner in 2008. (Photograph by the author.)

123

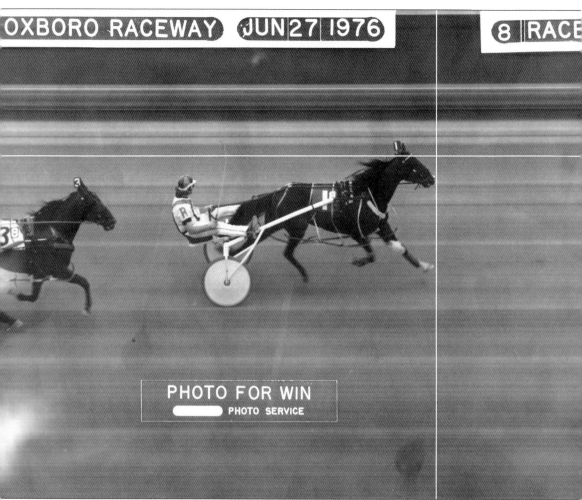

PHOTO FOR WIN
PHOTO SERVICE

Bay State Raceway was a harness racetrack in Foxborough. The track opened in 1947 and routinely packed in 10,000 people a night at its peak. But after a series of ownership changes in the 1970s and 1980s, the racetrack—then called New England Harness Raceway and later Foxboro Raceway and Foxboro Park—became tangled up with the history of the New England Patriots football team. In 1996, Patriots owner Robert Kraft purchased the racetrack and shut down horse racing at the site after a court battle. Foxboro Park closed in 1997 and was torn down in 2000 during the construction of Gillette Stadium, where the Patriots currently play. Former Foxboro Park general manager Gary Piontkowski set his sights on Plainville, just five miles south on Route 1, and opened Plainridge Racecourse in 1999. Plainridge now operates as Plainridge Park Casino. (Author's collection.)

Helen and Charles M. Nasif opened a modest dairy bar called Jolly Cholly's in North Attleborough in 1954. After they expanded the menu and hired roller-skating carhops, teenagers packed the place every Saturday night. In 1959, the Nasifs added an amusement park called Funland, best known for the giant clown sign that framed the entrance. Jolly Cholly's was sold in 1972. (Photograph by John Margolies, courtesy of LOC, LC-DIG-mrg-06719.)

Cowboy Town offered the "rootin . . . tootinest . . . time of your life" on Route 1 in Plainville from 1957 to 1960. Boston-area broadcaster Rex Trailer filmed some episodes of his long-running children's television show *Boomtown* at the Wild West theme park. Shown here is the Cowboy Town stagecoach making a promotional appearance at Fenway Park in Boston. (Courtesy of Plainville Historical Society.)

Mexican Patio Room   W   Route 1A. Rumford. R. I.   W   Banquet Hall

72658

Largest Diner In The World - Route 1, South Attleboro, Mas

Wightman's Diner called itself the largest diner in the world, and it is easy to see why. Elmer C. Wightman began with a 10-seat lunch wagon in South Attleboro in 1923. Over the next dozen years, he expanded the restaurant by stringing together multiple diner cars and adding a large dining room. Customers could choose among three dozen sandwiches—corned beef on rye was 15¢—or splurge on lobster with French fries and drawn butter for $1. John Wightman took over the business after his father's death in 1936 and ran the restaurant until he was drafted into the US Navy. Patronage declined while Wightman was away, and he closed the once-thriving spot in 1946. He salvaged fixtures from the diner and opened Johnnie's Tavern in Attleboro. (Courtesy of Tichnor/BPL.)

Pine Ridge Pet Cemetery is on the campus of the Animal Rescue League in Dedham, just a brief detour from Route 1. Established in 1907, the cemetery is the final resting place for about 20,000 animals. One monument honors "the many dogs that have given their lives in service to man." Also buried here is Igloo, the fox terrier that accompanied Adm. Richard Byrd on his polar expeditions. Iggy, as he was called, was so famous that he received an obituary in the *New York Times* when he died suddenly in 1931. And Pine Ridge shows the softer side of accused and acquitted axe murderer Lizzie Borden. Her three Boston terriers—Donald Stuart, Royal Nelson, and Laddie Miller—are buried in a quiet corner. (Photograph by the author.)

DISCOVER THOUSANDS OF LOCAL HISTORY BOOKS FEATURING MILLIONS OF VINTAGE IMAGES

Arcadia Publishing, the leading local history publisher in the United States, is committed to making history accessible and meaningful through publishing books that celebrate and preserve the heritage of America's people and places.

Find more books like this at
www.arcadiapublishing.com

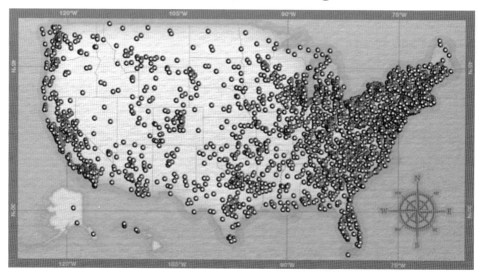

Search for your hometown history, your old stomping grounds, and even your favorite sports team.

Consistent with our mission to preserve history on a local level, this book was printed in South Carolina on American-made paper and manufactured entirely in the United States. Products carrying the accredited Forest Stewardship Council (FSC) label are printed on 100 percent FSC-certified paper.

MADE IN THE USA